CREATING
A
FUNCTIONAL BOARD

BRENDA KELLEHER-FLIGHT

BOARDROOM 101
RESOLVING COMMON BOARD ISSUES WITH THE DECISION
MAKING MODEL OF GOVERNANCE

THANK YOU

Thank you to my clients and my co-workers, without whom I could not have written this book. Board members asked hard questions. They required realistic answers and, in some cases, the know how to implement them. My intent is to address many of these typical boardroom dilemmas and, I hope, to make the lives of board members easier.

I am grateful to my husband who listens to me without judgement and patiently reads drafts of my thoughts. Also, a special thank you to Kathleen Davies, because she was patient, considerate, and thorough as she worked as the editor on the book.

Finally, thank you to you for taking the time to engage with this text. My thoughts and best wishes are with all board members, and I hope this content is useful in improving your board performance.

CONTENTS

PROLOGUE

This book is designed to make your life easier. Board governance is never meant to be difficult or stressful. Boards are designed to oversee their entity (not-for-profit, professional association, public-sector, council, association, or business) and ensure the mandates are achieved and their visions realized.

This book takes the mystic out of governance and addresses common issues faced by boards on a daily basis. It discusses how to identify gaps in your board's practices, and how to avoid common mistakes.

To ensure board members are content in their roles and each person understands the tasks delineated by the board and how to hold the Executive Director/CEO accountable, detailed information is provided. In creating *The Decision Making Model of Governance*, I aimed to demystify and make governance manageable, and that is my purpose with this guide to *Creating a Functional Board*.

By the end of this book, you will be more informed about how to keep your board work on track and create a positive legacy. My thoughts and best wishes are with you always.

Brenda Kelleher-Flight

.

1—WHY ARE SOME BOARDS DYSFUNCTIONAL?

BOARDS AND VALUE

Shareholders and stakeholders depend on their boards to make sound decisions after weighing all risks. Boards are designed to add value to organizations.

When they do not add value, it is because someone is not doing what needs to be done.

This chapter addresses the possible reasons:
1. Uninformed chairperson
2. Uncooperative board members
3. Uncommitted board members
4. Unclear mandate
5. Absence of clear board processes
6. Confusion between management and governance
7. Absence of governance policies
8. Presence of groupthink and absence of board evaluation.

UNINFORMED CHAIRPERSON

Nice people often get asked or selected to chair boards. Using this criterion is honorable; however, it should not rule out the other criteria.

Some of the needed attributes for effective chairpersons include the following:

- Knowledge of governance
- Understanding of what is required to ensure the board adds value
- Commitment to the board's mandate
- Willingness to ensure the board's constitution, bylaws, and/or governance policies are in place and followed
- Willingness to plan strategically and to act as a champion for the plan
- Ability to separate governance from management and to hold the CEO accountable for the management of the entity
- Ability to admit errors and take corrective action
- Willingness to have performance evaluated
- Skills to think and act from a win-win philosophy
- Ability to hold board members accountable for follow-through on their commitments, and
- Ability to deal with conflict of interest matters.

When a chair does not possess these attributes, it is essential for the board to have a plan in place to ensure this person has the opportunity to hone these skills.

UNCOOPERATIVE BOARD MEMBERS

Not all board members intend to be cooperative. They come to the board intending to prevent the board from taking a specific action, to promote their own agenda, or to try and convince the board to reverse a past decision.

These individuals can be difficult to deal with and can cause a major disruption to the board. The board needs clear policies and processes to ensure that these individuals do not disrupt the board's work and take the board off course.

The ways a board can do this include—

- Professional development in governance

- Review of its policies and why they exist

- Team building exercises

- Discussions about the effect of uncooperative board members on the board (a facilitator may be needed for this process)

- Use of the board's disciplinary process if the board member does not change his behavior

- Board member evaluations on a regular basis (every year, midterm, or every 18 months), and/or

- Alternate dispute resolution processes with a skilled facilitator.

UNCOMMITTED BOARD MEMBERS

There was a time when participation on a board was a good will gesture. People went, had tea, and were polite to each other. Many boards did not do any real work. This is no longer the case today, but there are still board members who go to board meetings when they can spare the time and have no real sense of commitment to the organization. How do you identify these members?

The signs include—

- Attend meetings sporadically

- Attend all meetings, but do not contribute

- Follow whatever processes they learned on other boards and do not question the validity of those practices

- Do not follow through on commitments

- Play down the importance of governance tasks and related issues

- Want to be buddies with the CEO and/or staff, and/or

- Avoid conflict at all costs.

Most boards appreciate individuals who are willing to run for election or accept appointments on boards. However, it is important that this acceptance is followed by commitment and dedication.

UNCLEAR MANDATE

Even the best board members lack direction when the board does not have a clear mandate.

Here is one exercise to try with your board:

> 1. Place board members in groups of two
>
> 2. Give each group a copy of the mandate
>
> 3. Ask each group to write their interpretation of the mandate on a flipchart based on—

- Who do we represent?

- What is the limit on our mandate?

- What are the lines of business this organization should offer?

- Are there any statements that are unclear, outdated, or unrelated to what this organization actually does?

- Is there a component of the organization's work missing?

> 4. When this exercise is complete, compare the answers to each question. Listen for similarities and differences.
>
> 5. Take the differences in interpretation and address each one until there is consensus.
>
> 6. Re-draft the mandate, or review the board's plan or work to ensure all aspects of the mandate are addressed.

It is important to ensure all board members are on the same page and the CEO is clear about what the entity is designed to accomplish.

The CEO should understand that he cannot limit or expand the lines of business without the permission of the board. When the lines are clear, the CEO is free to do his job without board interference.

ABSENCE OF CLEAR BOARD PROCESSES

It seems obvious that in any group where the members rotate there needs to be established processes to enable the group to work in harmony. This is not always the case.

ESTABLISHED PROCESSES ARE NEEDED TO ENABLE HARMONY

Topics will vary from board to board. Check your board's policies to see if the board's processes are clearly written or if they are passed on via word-of- mouth. Some topics to consider are—

- Attendance
- Board member orientation
- Code of ethics
- Confidentiality
- Policy development
- Professional development sessions/conferences and travel
- Public relations
- Quorum
- Scheduling, length and notice for regular board meetings
- Staff treatment
- Standards of behavior
- Succession planning
- Vacancies

Where board practices are not in writing, it may be helpful for the board, or its policy or governance committee, to do this.

CONFUSION BETWEEN MANAGEMENT AND GOVERNANCE

It is difficult to answer the question, "What is governance?" While the tasks are clear, the boundaries differ from entity to entity based on the number of staff, the way the entity was established, regulatory requirements, and the amount of trust between the board and the CEO.

There are key questions the board can ask itself:

- Is the mandate clear?

- Are the lines of business clear?

- Do we have a vision and mission?

- Do we have clear governance policies?

- Are there clear management policies?

- How many employees does the board have reporting directly to it?

- Are the roles of the board, its members, its officers, and the CEO clear and different from each other?

Each time an issue arises, the board asks questions such as—

- What aspect of this issue is governance?

- Who is responsible to deal with this issue, the board or the CEO?

- Should the board get involved at this stage or remain one step away in the event the issue cannot be resolved?

- Based on our organizational chart, who should deal with this issue?

If a board does not stop and question who should handle each issue, it will deal with anything and everything that comes its way, whether or not it is governance. The board may be an excellent buffer if an issue cannot be resolved by the CEO; however, if it becomes involved too early, it can set itself up for failure. It may not be viewed as impartial or trustworthy by stakeholders.

ABSENCE OF GOVERNANCE POLICIES

Consistency and clarity are essential to all governance practices. A board cannot afford to shift and change each time a new member joins the board or a new chair is selected. It is critical for board members to feel safe and know that its practices are based on a solid foundation. That foundation is the governance policies of the board.

The Decision Making Model of Governance suggests that boards consider policies in nine areas:

1. Board processes
2. Accountability
3. Representation
4. Finances
5. Evaluation (board, board members, and CEO)
6. Planning
7. Outcomes for lines of business
8. Risks
9. Roles and Responsibilities

It is easy for a board to be dysfunctional when its policies are unclear. Board members and the CEO are left without a clear guide for actions and limitations.

PRESENCE OF GROUPTHINK AND ABSENCE OF BOARD EVALUATION

It is nice to say 'we all get along and everything is great,' but is it reality? Trouble happens to good people when they are hoodwinked into thinking in unison and risks are not addressed. It is not essential for all board members to think alike. However, it is vital for all board members to support board decisions.

IT IS VITAL FOR ALL BOARD MEMBERS TO SUPPORT BOARD DECISIONS

There is a difference between the following statements:

The board made that decision, but I don't agree with it.

The decision of the board is this... . If you have an objection to it, you can... (add the best ending for your situation):

- Bring it to the attention of X

- I can bring it to his attention for you

- You can follow the board's appeal process, which is a, b, and c.

Boards that engage in groupthink often adopt a 'we-they' way of thinking. This is not the most beneficial stance for boards. In fact, such boards may fail to add value to the entity or to leave a positive legacy.

If the board does not evaluate its performance it may remain dysfunctional, thereby leaving a poor legacy for new members to follow. The reality for a new board may be that it has to do a considerable amount of foundational work before it can begin to govern effectively.

Open discussion—presentation of multiple viewpoints, disagreement, evaluation of risks, and comparison of options to the vision and mission of the organization—is very healthy.

MOVING TO EXCELLENCE

Boards can move from dysfunction to excellence in governance. It does take work and commitment, but it is possible. To move to excellence, support the chairperson, ask all board members to cooperate, and choose committed directors. Ensure you outline a clear mandate, adopt clear board processes, clarify the lines between management and governance, adopt governance policies, and expect diverse opinions, evaluate risks, and evaluate the board's effectiveness.

2—THE BASICS

THE FIVE BOARD 'MUSTS'

Board governance is not easily defined. What is required in one situation may not be appropriate in another. Many factors affect good board governance and governance is not a thing, but a process. What are the basics that boards must know or do to manage the job effectively and fulfill obligations and expectations?

BASICS OF GOOD GOVERNANCE

Decision making is the key underlying element of good governance and must be integrated with the process. For decision making to occur in a timely and efficient manner, different individuals with a multitude of styles, experiences, agendas, and expertise are expected to come together and work as a team.

To make this likely, boards need to understand five key aspects of governance: board authority, what leadership means in this context, board responsibilities, how to plan effectively, and what it means to be accountable.

BOARDS NEED TO ACCEPT AUTHORITY

Board members need to be able to answer the following:

- What is the legal authority divested to the board?

- Are there limits?

- Does the board have authority over the organization and the resources?

- Are there specific processes the board must follow in making certain decisions?

For example, a public body may have to seek permission from the specific government that set it up prior to making decisions that could have political or financial implications.

A not-for-profit board may have to seek permission from its members prior to invoking policy changes that could impact the membership.

A private company may have to seek the permission of its shareholder in specific cases that could affect the shareholder returns on investment.

A board of a professional association may have to seek membership input prior to making changes to member benefits or standards of practice.

BOARDS NEED TO BE LEADERS

Often, boards are expected to reflect the values and priorities of their owners. The question is whether these values and priorities are clearly stated and understood. If not, then the board has the task of defining its values and outlining its strategic directions.

Leadership has many facets. It requires the board to connect with those it represents, whom it must guide, and those to whom it is accountable.

In order to do this successfully, it is essential for boards to be

- Able to see the big picture

- Committed to the roles, responsibilities, and mandate of the entity

- Willing to listen actively

- Able to communicate openly, honestly, and in a timely manner

- Able to maintain focus on issues and remain detached from personal comments or needs

- Goal-oriented and refrain from changing directions mid-stream without good reason, solve conflicts as soon as possible, and maintain respect for all involved in the goal-setting process

- Well-read, which means gleaning information from various sources/not just the CEO, determining where there are gaps, and formulating questions to access data to fill those gaps, and

- Willing to maintain confidentiality and let governance processes take their course, while honoring the role of the board's spokesperson.

When members demonstrate these leadership qualities—needed to fulfill their roles effectively—they are ready to function as a team and accept the conferred responsibilities.

BOARDS NEED TO BE RESPONSIBLE AGENTS

In theory, boards are assigned a mandate. However, those mandates are not clearly defined in many cases, with the result that the boards can shift, based on the desires of its members. Boards as responsible agents need to ensure the mandate is defined and set clear parameters.

WHEN MANDATES ARE NOT CLEAR... PROBLEMS ENSUE

When the mandates are not clear, several problems can ensue. Boards are unable to focus on any aspect of their perceived mandates. As a result, nothing is accomplished. Boards modify what they perceive to be their mandates and cause confusion. They are unable to maintain directions:

- Unable to be a champion for all of their initiatives

- Do not complete their own governance functions because they are always shifting focus

- Are unable to explain how they are different from other boards, and

- Become splintered or cannot find the funds to do everything they want to do.

When reviewing their mandate, boards need to ask certain specific questions:

- What is this board expected to achieve?

- Is this board expected to serve any particular population, area, or sector?

- What are our sources of funding and does/should this limit the role?

- Are there other entities doing any of the functions we want to do?

- Are we following a business model or a social-sector model?

- Could we do what we want to do even if we had maximum resources?

- What would the board like to accomplish, and is this different from what the board could accomplish—given its resources?

Boards need to be realistic. Governance takes time and energy. Employees only have so much time and so many resources. Deciding what your board can realistically accomplish, short and long-term, is critical. Once those decisions are made, boards are expected to accept the responsibilities assigned. Board members are required to devote their personal time, energy, and expertise to ensure the board achieves its mission and mandate. This means planning effectively.

BOARDS NEED TO BE PLANNERS

Set standards that determine what needs to be accomplished by specific deadlines. For business boards and member associations, this means determining what value creation looks like in your particular situation.

All boards need to evaluate what is happening in society at large and the impact of new innovations, new networks, current public policies, and potential risks.

When planning, be aware that it is imperative that targets and time frames be realistic and achievable.

Boards determine when and how to monitor progress and are aware of the person or group assigned responsibility for taking any needed corrective action. They are cognizant that unplanned risks and opportunities will arise, which are impossible to anticipate. This is not a negative reflection on the boards, when they do their jobs thoroughly.

When the board members fulfill their roles, the board is ready to demonstrate accountability to the moral and legal owners.

BOARDS NEED TO BE ACCOUNTABLE

It is also the boards that hold the CEOs accountable for their assigned responsibilities. They do not allow CEOs to shift responsibilities onto the boards, make excuses for non-performance, justify re-routing resources without permission, or focus on favorite/select areas within the organization.

Each board needs to answer for the discharge of its assigned responsibilities. As the bodies that know what needs to be accomplished by when and by whom, boards ensure the resources are assigned in the right areas. They report to shareholders, owners, or members for the results achieved.

FAILURE MAY HAVE MAJOR IMPLICATIONS FOR THE ORGANIZATION

Boards need to determine how often and how to report on their accomplishments, how to let others know about good news within the organization, and the challenges that may present in the future.

Five prime areas that boards need to do well relate to authority, leadership, responsibilities, planning, and accountability.

If any fail in these areas, it may have major implications for the organization and for upcoming boards. It's key that your board focuses on each area, determines what needs to be done to fulfill governance responsibilities, plans to ensure diligence and attention to detail, and measures your success.

3 —MYTHS ABOUT GOVERNANCE BOARDS

EXPECTATIONS AND HOW TO MEET THEM

What are your board's expectations? Do you tell board members essential information or do they learn as they go? Unfortunately, many board members learn as they attend board meetings. The CEO provides an overview of the organization and, perhaps, a thick binder of materials. New directors wonder if (and when) they will find time to read it.

Many individuals say they were on their boards a year or more before they fully understood what was going on and what was expected. Seven beliefs that can lead to poor governance practices are highlighted in this chapter. Methods to avoid such errors in judgement are included.

1—BOARD MEMBERS ARE FAMILIAR WITH THE DIFFERENT MODELS OF GOVERNANCE.

The following 11 models are typically used by boards:

- Advisory

- Agency or corporate

- Charismatic

- Collective

- Management
- Representational
- Results-oriented
- Traditional
- Working
- Policy Governance
- Decision Making Model of Governance.

Only two are fully developed—Policy Governance and The Decision Making Model of Governance. Review both and choose the model that best suits your mandate.

2—BOARD MEMBERS UNDERSTAND THE DIFFERENCE BETWEEN GOVERNANCE AND MANAGEMENT.

My research determined that the distinction is not clear. Boards need to set aside time to address the difference between their responsibilities and those of the CEO in the eight essential areas of mandate, lines of business, policies, fiscal management, planning, risk management, representation, and accountability. The key difference is that the board looks outward, while the CEO looks inward.

3—BOARD MEMBERS LEARN ABOUT THE BOARD, ITS ROLE, AND THE BOARD LIMITATIONS BY ATTENDING MEETINGS.

The hazard to this approach is that it can take a long time to gain comprehensive knowledge. Yet it is critical that directors understand and accept their governance role and the limitations established in the boards' mandate, sooner rather than later.

When it takes up to a year or more to learn the governance role (the average quoted), about a third of the members' term can be over before they are able to contribute effectively to board deliberations, risk analysis, and decision making. Board members have a right to access information and opportunities and have questions answered in a timely manner on the following areas—this will enhance productivity and achievement:

- Appeals processes
- Applicable legislation or policies of other bodies that directly influence actions of the board
- Conflict resolution strategies or processes
- Meetings, purposes, and rules of order
- Representation responsibilities.
- The board's constitution, bylaws, and policies
- The communications processes and plan
- The mandate and lines of business of the board
- The role of individual board members
- The role of sub-committees, if they exist
- The role of the board
- The role of the board in budgeting and finances
- The role of the board in collective bargaining
- The role of the CEO
- The role of the chairperson of the board if he acts as more than a facilitator of meetings
- The standards of behavior, codes of conduct, and
- The strategic planning process and associated accountability responsibilities.

4—BOARD MEMBERS WILL AUTOMATICALLY EMBRACE THEIR GOVERNANCE ROLE.

Various aspects of board governance are unfamiliar and certain parts of the governance role, such as risk oversight, policy development, and strategic planning, may not be as interesting as many areas of management.

This focus on management issues occurs for several reasons. Many stakeholders insist that board members are responsible for addressing their concerns and such concerns relate to management. These include areas such as staffing, organizational rules, and organization-stakeholder relations.

Specific members may wish to prevent the board from repeating a decision similar to one made in the past. They may want information accessible only to management because that information could influence their business or other organizations to which they belong.

Members may believe that they need to know everything that is going on inside the organization in order to govern. They may not trust others to make decisions in their favor or feel the CEO is competent.

They may see their role on the board as a stepping stone to other opportunities and believe they need to spend time furthering an agenda. Finally, they may not have the time needed to learn the role.

5—IT IS NOT NECESSARY TO REVEAL WHY AN INDIVIDUAL ACCEPTED A POSITION ON YOUR BOARD.

The decision making process can be influenced when a board member's motives are misinterpreted. As well as misunderstandings, this leads to the formation of splinter groups, and the utilization of personal or professional associations to pressure the board to make or modify specific decisions.

Openness and transparency are necessary to build an effective board-governance team. All agendas must be placed on the table. In reality, many board members know their peers' agendas, even when they are not overtly stated. However, there is room for these to be misunderstood or misinterpreted when not clearly outlined.

6—IT IS NOT NECESSARY FOR A BOARD TO SET ITS OWN AGENDA.

Dissension among the board members may result if a board leaves the task of setting the agenda to the CEO or the CEO and/or board chair. Certain board members may—

- Feel they are unable get their items placed on the agenda and resent those board members who are successful

- Think that all of the power rests with the board chair, or the board chair and CEO, and fail to believe that the board operates as a team

- Believe that the board is being run by the CEO and the board chair is just a figure head, and

- Think that all the key discussions occur prior to the board meeting and their purpose is to rubber stamp what the CEO and/or CEO and board chair decide.

Governance boards can change this by deciding what information they need and when, and also what decisions they need to make once they have the information. Then they can begin to draft agendas for the full year:

- Ensuring decision making items that were not handled are placed immediately on the next agenda

- Ensuring that board members have ample opportunity to suggest items and note whether these items are for information purposes, whether advice is sought, or whether the board needs to make decisions, and

- Asking advisory groups or committees to place their motion topics on the agendas rather than stating 'committee report.'

GIVE BOARD MEMBERS TIME TO REVIEW ISSUES PRIOR TO MEETINGS

This would give board members an opportunity to review issues prior to attending a meeting.

7—IT IS NOT NECESSARY TO PRIORITIZE AGENDA ITEMS.

Most boards have packed agendas. Meeting time is limited. The first item of business should be to determine the items of business placed on the agenda for information purposes only, which are there because the advice of the board is sought, and which require a decision. Items that require decisions should be dealt with before the end of a meeting.

Prioritize as follows:

Decision items are first priority and handled prior to the end of the meeting. These items are within the board's sphere of control.

Advice items are given second priority and the board recognizes it is only one source of advice, thus any input may not be the decision taken by the person seeking the advice. These items are within the board's sphere of influence only.

Information items are given the lowest priority. Boards cannot influence these items. Therefore, directors could be provided with handouts to read at a later time. It is easy for a board to be upset about someone else's decision or policy and waste time discussing the impact on the board or organization. At the end of the day, nothing is going to change.

IN SUMMARY

Board members need to understand what is going on and what is expected of them. The following avoids the seven beliefs that can lead to poor governance practices and errors in judgement:

- Give board members information about the different models of governance and the one your board uses

- Ensure board members understand the difference between governance and management

- Provide a comprehensive orientation

- Ensure members understand and accept their governance role

- Understand why board members accepted a position on your board

- Ensure the board sets its own agenda, and

- Prioritize agenda items.

4—HOW TO AVOID THE NINE MOST COMMON BOARD MISTAKES

FOUNDATIONS FOR FUNCTIONALITY

Boards serve a critical function—protecting the public good by listening to citizens—and making prudent decisions while focusing on the outcomes desired for their public/s.

From time to time, boards find they are unable to function as the effective teams they need to be to achieve mandates. When a board knows and is able to use the right tools to identify and address underlying issues, board productivity is one of the benefits.

MISTAKE #1— FAILING TO CHOOSE A MODEL OF GOVERNANCE

It's useful to examine two fully developed models of governance—the PolicyGovernance® model developed by John Carver (1997) in his book titled *Boards That Make a Difference: A New Design for Leadership in Nonprofit and Public Organizations* and *The Decision Making Model of Governance* developed by your author (please see *The Productive Boardroom*). The differences between the two models are shown in the following chart. Either of the two models, or a combination, may meet your board's needs. Review and determine which is more applicable, and then follow as closely as possible.

	Models	
	Policy Governance®	DecisionMaking
1. Who does work	Board governs. Staff do their own work.	Board, in collaboration with all owners, creates the circumstances necessary to achieve the agreed upon vision and mission. Boards govern and staff operate the organization.
2. Who governs	Board through policies.	All external stakeholders via the board. The board plans, clarifies the mandate and lines of business, negotiates outcomes, oversees finances and risk, develops policy, monitors progress, and evaluates the board's and the organization's success.
3. Level of Staffing	Depends on organization	Has a CEO and many staff.
4. Decision Making	Majority rule: board unanimity crucial	Majority rule after the opinions of all key stakeholder have been sought. Members represent all stakeholders and know who will benefit and who will be marginalized.
5. Policy Areas	Ends; Executive Limitations; Board-Executive Relationship; and Board Process (Carver, 1997, p.34)	Board processes. Roles and responsibilities of the board, its members and the CEO; Well-being outcomes desired for the lines of business; Evaluation processes; Fiscal oversight; Planning; Risk management; Representation; and Accountability.
6. Accountability	Accountability is seen as the "responsibility that accumulates" (Carver, 1997, p.105)	Accountability is seen as including the moral and legal owners in a participative manner; designing program and policy strategies around negotiated settlements; answering for assigned responsibilities; and being transparent in all activities, unless there is a legal reason prohibiting such action.
7. Representation	Moral ownership rather than legal ownership is the basis on which a board determines its accountability (Carver, 1997, p.121).	The board represents the moral (citizens) and the legal owners, and values personal experiences and field-specific expertise equally.
8. Evaluation	Of the CEO via the CEO limitation and ends policies	Of the board as a whole, each board member and the CEO

When a board of directors fails to select a model, or design one of its own, its operations are typically based on the wishes (or whims) of current board members. To be effective, your chosen model should stand the test of time and enable new members to become familiar with operations quickly, thereby avoiding a negative impact on productivity. Working with an accepted model also gives the board confidence that successive board chairs or CEOs will maintain it, enhancing operational continuity.

MISTAKE #2— FAILING TO CHOOSE A PROCESS TO SEPARATE GOVERNANCE FROM MANAGEMENT

Governance is not management. Governance is the obligation to engage in dialogue and make decisions:

- Clarifying the mandate of the organization

- Ensuring the lines of business and their parameters are responsive to the citizens' or clients' needs and board's resource realities

- Developing, implementing, monitoring, and evaluating governance policies

- Governing within the entity's fiscal envelope

- Representing all primary stakeholders

- Determining and overseeing risks

- Planning strategically at the governance level, and

- Demonstrating that accountability responsibilities are fulfilled by reporting on the program outcomes, fiscal proprieties and legal obligations.

Management is the obligation to undertake the following:

- Dialogue and make policies that influence day-to-day decisions within the organization

- Establish procedures to direct routine transactions and normal operations of the organization related to fiscal management, risk management, programs, and human resources while ensuring they are within the governance policies

- Confirm that programs, services, and products offered are within the parameters set by the board

- Identify and address internal risks

- Ensure internal stakeholders' voices are heard, and

- Report to the board as required.

MANAGEMENT POLICIES INFLUENCE DAY-TO-DAY DECISIONS

MISTAKE #3— FAILING TO KNOW THE BOARD'S ROLE REGARDING EACH AGENDA ITEM

It is easy for a board to spend considerable amounts of scarce board meeting time discussing items outside of its control, outside its sphere of influence, or inside the role of management.

One of the ways to ensure this does not happen to your board is to classify items as information, advice, or decision making.

Information-class items on the agenda do not need to be discussed because the board cannot change the situation. The item is placed on the agenda to inform the board and any time taken by discussion will not alter the actuality. Commenting on these items can take place informally over coffee or lunch.

THE BOARD IS SEEN AS ONE VALUABLE SOURCE OF INPUT

Items classified under advice are there because the board is seen as one valuable source of input prior to a decision being made by the CEO or by another group. The important point for the board to remember is that it is giving advice. The recipient may not follow this advice.

I have noted that board members may become frustrated or disappointed if the CEO or the individual who sought their advice did not follow it.

Remember that the board may be only one of the sources of advice the recipient pursues. As a result, the board's advice may be not used at all, be used in concert with other advice, or as it was presented. When the board was asked for advice, it was not making a decision. It was offering an opinion.

The third class of item on board agendas falls under governance and require a decision. It is essential for the board to give these items the highest priority.

These items should meet the following criteria:

- Not fall within the mandate of management

- Be (clearly) within the role of the board

- Not relate to rules required to run the day-to-day operations of the organization

- Relate to outcomes and not means

- Affect the outcomes for the moral (clients) or the legal owners (funders) of the organization, and

- Be within the sphere of control or influence of the board.

MISTAKE #4— FAILING TO FOLLOW APPROVED POLICIES

It is essential that all directors have a thorough understanding of the board's constitution, bylaws, and policies. It is critical for the board chair to ensure that each option under consideration is in harmony with board policies. When an idea contravenes one of the current policies, the board must make its final decision in full knowledge that it is circumventing policy. In those cases, the board can override the old policy and insert the new decision as the new policy. Where the new decision contravenes the board's constitution or bylaws, it is incumbent upon the board chairperson to follow the process for revising the constitution or bylaws.

A board member often requests a change in a policy when feeling pressured by a special interest group. She may feel obligated to act for the wishes of the organization that asked her to represent it on the board.

She may have joined the board—

- To ensure a specific policy was changed

- Because she believes that her best interests or the best interests of those close to her would be better served by a different policy, or

- Thinks that a policy is outdated and no longer serves the best interests of the users or owners.

When considering making a decision in contravention of its own policy/ies, it is important for the board, as a whole, to evaluate—

- Each potential decision against its current constitution, bylaws, and policies

- The risks associated with changing a current policy
- The unintended outcomes that could potentially be associated with such a decision
- The impact on marginalized persons/groups, and
- The long-term consequences of changing the policy.

When considering policy change, also examine whether—

- Board level is where the decision should be made
- It's an outcome
- The board should absolutely be concerned with the means or 'how' decisions
- It is concise and inclusive of all the relevant factors the board must take into account
- Written in a manner that cannot be misinterpreted and sets limits
- Identifies those in the system affected
- Indicates costs where applicable
- Effectiveness can be measured, and
- The entity has the power and resources to implement it.

MISTAKE #5— EMPOWERING SUB-COMMITTEES TO MAKE DECISIONS ON BEHALF OF THE BOARD

Committees do not fulfill a beneficial function when they—

- Make routine decisions for the board
- Make decisions that are within the role of senior management personnel, or

- Present recommendations to the board.

A committee would not make

routine decisions on behalf of the full board. Unless there are time constraints, imminent risks, or long-term consequences associated with leaving a decision until the next board meeting, there's no reason for the committee to make a decision.

When a committee is dependent upon a senior management employee to generate its agendas and bring forth information, the committee is most likely making decisions that fall within the purview of management.

It is vital that committees generate their own agenda, question all agenda items to ensure they are governance tasks, and meet without relying on staff.

Committee members should not be concerned with circumventing (or annihilating) fellow board members. However, this does occur when board committees bring forward recommendations without explaining the options they examined and the risks associated with the options.

Board members may be reluctant to question their colleagues and friends who sit on committees, fearing such questions will be interpreted as mistrust. They also know that the support of the committee members may be crucial when issues they are concerned about come forward.

Committees play a vital role when—

- Boards are unable to meet on a frequent basis because of geography or financial constraints

- Emergency decisions need to be made between meetings and not all board members can accommodate emergency sessions, and

- For information gathering, which is time consuming—so a select group/committee undertakes research, develops options, documents risks, and outlines the pros and cons associated with each option for board consideration.

MISTAKE # 6—FAILURE TO ACKNOWLEDGE THE AGENDAS OF INDIVIDUAL BOARD MEMBERS

Directors agree to serve on a board for a variety of reasons.

Therefore, it's essential that each individual feels free to state her agenda. Individuals agree to serve—

- To make a contribution to the well-being of the citizens in a particular community, zone, or sub-region within the board

- To contribute to the well-being of all citizens within the geographical boundaries covered by the board

- To ensure that the board does not repeat a decision similar to one it made in the past

- To make certain that the board does not reduce or remove services from a particular community

- To convince the board to introduce or increase accessibility to a specific program, service, or product

- To protect the interests of another group, such as a town council, association, special interest group, or union

- To try and stop the board from making a specific decision

- To gain credentials

- To fulfill political or professional aspirations

- To meet a personal need

- To contribute a specific set of skills

- As a favor for another person or group

- To gain a specific set of skills, or

- To have access to specific perks, such as travel or professional development.

When free to be open about their reasons for joining, it is easier for board members to participate in discussions and beneficial for fellow members. Each is aware of the others' frames of reference on issues and arguments.

It also enhances the learning curve. Members learn what evidence to present to counterparts, how to present arguments, and the barriers in place that could prevent selection of their options when motions are put to a vote.

MISTAKE #7— FAILING TO SPECIFY WHEN BOARD MEMBERS CAN SPEAK ON BEHALF OF THE BOARD

Rarely do board policies cover under what circumstances directors may speak for the board. However, because of their board membership they are expected to give speeches at board events, meet with community representatives, regional/town councils and many other groups.

As policy, members should attend these functions with access to a script prepared and approved by the board, be able to restate the board's position on issues, and listen.

The best boards address these questions:

- Under what circumstances can board members meet with stakeholders without the permission of the full board?

- Can board members enter facilities or sites without board permission? If they do, whom do they represent?

- When can a board member offer their opinions in forums other than board meetings?

It is embarrassing for a board member to discover that she erred when, on being asked for an opinion, she was expected to confirm the stance of the board only or acknowledge that a decision had not yet been made.

To avoid misunderstandings, write limitations as policy:

- When she can speak on behalf of the board

- When she can meet with stakeholders and freely offer her opinions

- When she can enter facilities/sites and gather information as a representative of the board, and

- When she can openly divulge what happened at a board meeting or disclose decisions made by the board to the group she represents.

MISTAKE #8— FAILING TO HAVE A GOVERNANCE PLAN THAT IS ACHIEVABLE WITHIN CURRENT RESOURCE ALLOCATIONS

Why do boards spend valuable time designing plans that they know they will never fulfill? How does a wish list help? Wouldn't it be better to spend time designing a plan that's achievable, given the stated timelines, current fiscal resources of the board, its current human resources, and current mandate?

Most board members are busy people. They do not have time to produce documents that will be filed and never used. The board is responsible for achieving outcomes. It is critical that it focus on specific priorities, make decisions based on those priorities, and act as a champion for those priorities.

IT IS CRITICAL THAT THE BOARD FOCUS ON SPECIFIC PRIORITIES

To ensure that the plan the board develops is useful, it is important it meets specific criteria.

Before approving, the board would ensure the following:

- The plan specifies the evidence the board will use to determine if goals and objectives are met

- The plan specifies when the board expects updates regarding progress

- Ensures the fiscal, physical, and human resources to successfully fulfill the goals and objectives in the plan

- Includes the lines of business and parameters that would limit the work of senior staff

- Includes measurable targets

- Has the mechanisms in place to collect the data it requires

- Puts the mechanisms in place to ensure it is notified when the data collected indicates targets will not be met, and

- Polls board members to ensure they are willing and able to fulfill board commitments outlined in the plan.

MISTAKE #9— ASSUMING BOARD MEMBERS UNDERSTAND THE ROLES THEY ARE EXPECTED TO FULFILL

Too many individuals state that they ran for election or accepted a board appointment, yet lack clarity about the role of a board member. They attend meetings and participate in discussions, but they are not sure if they are doing what they are supposed to do, which includes the following tasks:

- Decision making

- Finances

- Risk management

- Communication

- Planning, monitoring, and reporting

- Collective bargaining

- Policy development and implementation

- Board evaluation

- Board member evaluation

- CEO evaluation, and

- Representing the board.

Governance models should also address and be of value in determining and describing the following:

- The role of the board chair

- The role of the board committees

- The role of the CEO

- The rules of order used during meetings

- The standards of behavior

- The code of ethics

- The board's mandate

- Where the mandate of the board meets/conflicts the mandate of other boards

- Areas that are not the mandate of the board, but of special interest to the board member

- The role of the board executive

- Constitution, bylaws, and policies

- Conflict of interest limitations, and

- When the board member can and cannot represent the board.

5—IDENTIFYING GAPS IN BOARD PRACTICE

AIMING FOR EXCELLENCE

Excellence in governance requires boards to oversee their organizations from several perspectives. These include visioning and strategic planning, risk oversight, representation, financial accountability, evaluation, and CEO succession planning.

Unfortunately, not all directors receive professional development in the area of governance. These board members may have influential roles and believe they are governing effectively. However, they may either be managing or acting in the stead of staff and be, in actuality, micromanaging.

This chapter examines the underlying issues and the significance of each of the named components of governance and the gaps that occur when boards or board members manage or micromanage.

UNDERLYING ISSUES

For boards to be visionary, govern effectively, and plan for the future, they must determine their role. An ill-defined role delivers many different results.

This section examines the role of the board as visionary, manager, and field-specific experts. If you're not certain what definition fits your board, consider the questions that might relate.

BOARD AS A VISIONARY

When boards act with vision, they are concerned with the following questions:

- Will the model of governance we are using provide consistent value to our stakeholders (clients, users, patients, customers, employees, vendors, and lenders) beyond what they state they expect?

- Can the model provide guidance to board members who may join the board without any governance experience?

- Does our model demonstrate exceptional organization, order, and respect for culture?

- Are the board processes outlined in detail for future boards?

- Does the model of governance provide uniformly predictable access, services, and programs for our clients or customers?

- Does this model utilize a set of values, a code of ethics, and standards of behavior that are observable and consistent to our clients, users, patients, customers, employees, vendors, and lenders?

When boards ask such questions, members tend to realize their positions are temporary and they have a role to fulfill. They understand that, during their tenure, their role is to ensure that the CEO can function effectively in their absence and clients/customers are treated consistently, based on a set of measurable standards.

BOARD AS A MANAGER

When boards act as managers, they are focused on the following:

- Will the model of governance we use ensure we understand what the CEO and his team are doing?

- Isn't it okay to accept the notion that this model is our model of governance and any new members or a new CEO can shape the way the board operates, based on their strengths?

- Isn't it correct to believe that the CEO is responsible for the culture and values within the organization and we do not need to be organized for the CEO to be organized?

- Our policies do not need to be measurable and reviewed regularly; wouldn't we refer to them when we need them?

- Why should a board wonder whether there is uniformly predictable access, services, and programs for our clients, users, patients, or customers?

- We know our values; why would we write them down or need to know them off the top of our heads?

When board members think this way, they may become heavily reliant on the CEO. The CEO finds he or she needs to keep on the board's side to ensure it does not intrude too much in management issues. Boards often trust the CEO completely and refrain from questioning his judgement.

On the other hand, the board might find that its agenda is full of management items and rarely does it focus on governance issues. When the board is managing, it means the board members are more comfortable with management than governance. They find it necessary to oversee all CEO responsibilities, in the task of 'ensuring we are informed' or 'representing our stakeholders.'

BOARD AS FIELD-SPECIFIC EXPERTS

When boards act as field-specific experts, they may relate from this self-defined viewpoint and focus on the following:

- Will the model of governance we are using provide an opportunity for me to demonstrate my expertise?

- Why would a model provide guidance to board members who would join the board without any governance experience?

- Does our model demonstrate exceptional organization and order in the area that is of specific interest to me?

- Are the board processes related to decision making, problem solving, roles, etc., outlined as my profession would expect?

- Isn't my role to ensure that the items within my area of expertise are in good order?

- Why would I need values, a code of ethics, and standards of behavior when I already have those in my profession?

These board members want to do their own thing. They do not want other board members to assume any aspect of their role that is congruent with their professional expertise. For example, you will hear a board member say, "I've been on the finance committee for years. That's my expertise. I'm not interested in serving on any other committee." These board members tend to focus on finances during board meetings and rarely contribute to the other discussions.

Board members need to be knowledgeable in all areas of governance in order for the board to function as a team and speak with one voice.

ACTING ON INFORMATION

To make decisions, boards require reliable information that is current and specific to the topic at hand. Boards cannot sit on the fence. A board's role is to make decisions on all governance items and either accept a motion, defer it, or deny it.

Information is essential, but much of the knowledge required may not be available in a reliable form on demand. As a result, boards must pause to consider the options and determine whether to forge ahead or postpone a decision until the information is obtained.

Another related issue is the ability of the gate keepers, usually the CEOs, to filter the information and provide their boards with only the input they believe to be relevant. This means that it may be consciously or unconsciously withheld—i.e., when the information is not conducive to producing the decision CEOs desire.

A third issue relates to board structure. Where committees exist, the board committee may filter the information presented to the board. When this happens, board members can either decide to 'trust' or 'question' the committee members. This may leave the impression that fellow directors do not appreciate the committee members' hard work or else question their judgement.

Excellence in governance depends on quality information that is reliable and not filtered, unless necessarily and transparently. Essential information presents all risks and options available to the boards, with the associated pros and cons.

When a board fails to recognize that the CEO controls the information it receives and blindly accepts what it is given, it is not governing.

WHEN BOARDS HAVE VISION

When boards have a clear vision, they see the customer/client as an opportunity. They accept the past, work in the present, and focus on the future.

They know the values the entity must demonstrate and practice those values in all actions and reactions.

They refuse to manage and have effective mechanisms in place to ensure the CEOs do the managing. They implement governance policies that are timeless, measurable, and realistic.

These boards know whom they represent and understand their legal obligations. They are never controlled by the whim of the current board members. The standards such boards establish apply now and into the future.

PLANNING STRATEGICALLY

When plans are strategic, they are futuristic in their aims. The goals are directed toward the missions and visions. Resources are dedicated to the fulfillment of the plans and the boards are the plans' champions.

When boards are not strategic, they complete a plan, forget about it, and assume it is the CEO's role to ensure the goals are met. Boards are too busy with the tasks of the day to focus on the future or their visions.

RISK AND RISK AVOIDANCE

Gaps occur when boards fail to identify risks. Board members say, "We talked about the issue." Yet they can't answer the key question, "What are the specific risks?" The board's role is to identify risks and determine whether they can take the risks or mitigate them.

Risks become reality when boards make decisions without examining the possibilities and then have to scramble to deal with the fallout. By then, it's too late.

It is essential for boards to close the gap by clearly identifying the potential repercussions and the steps they would take in the event of such repercussions occurring.

REPRESENTATION

Gaps occur when board members are unsure of whom they represent. Are board members, who represent themselves, always cognizant of and viewing their work from the perspective of their professional backgrounds?

It is possible for board members to represent opinions without being ombudsmen for any person or group?

Working through the questions and answers provides the vehicle for boards to identify whether they represent any or all of the following:

- Compliance organizations
- Vendors
- Shareholders
- Users

- Staff, or

- Business.

Prior to making decisions, it is essential that boards identify key stakeholders. If they do not, they are at the whim of everyone with whom they interact.

FINANCIAL OVERSIGHT

Certain boards have very little need for financial oversight because they are controlled by an external owner or authority. For example, public-sector boards may find that their accounting methods, quarterly financial statements, and audits are overseen by their governments, with very little left to the discretion of the boards.

BOARDS MAY HAVE NO ONE TO OVERSEE THEIR FINANCIAL HEALTH

In these cases, boards are often left to focus on minute details. Oversight may be unnecessary on a monthly or quarterly basis.

Other boards have no one to oversee their financial health. When not-for-profit entities function without a budget, it is clear that they view their work in the short-term only.

In fact, it is vital that such boards focus on the future and develop a strategy to secure the finances needed for this future. While this is occurring, the boards develop methods to ensure finances are used as intended, illegal activity does not occur, and financial risks are uncovered as soon as possible.

EVALUATE EFFECTIVENESS

Are board roles defined? In many cases, the answer is no. Gaps occur in the absence of definitions, with the result that directors are not oriented to the limits of their roles when they assume membership.

In these cases, strong individuals can shift the boards' agendas and derail positive advances toward the vision. It is incumbent that boards/members know their roles, their legal obligations, and how well they are fulfilling responsibilities because, in short, this shows how well they are governing.

To evaluate effectiveness of the board of directors, it is important to seek outside support. Self-evaluations may over-inflate the positive aspects of the board or, conversely, be swayed by one or two negative voices.

BOARDS THAT MISS THE POINT

Gaps occur (i) when boards do not take the time to determine what governance means in the context of their organization, (ii) when they do not know the possible models of governance or if/how and when to apply them, and (iii) when they focus on the small stuff. Boards are unable to concentrate sufficiently on the future to make their present efforts effective.

6—EVALUATING YOUR BOARD

WHY YOU SHOULD

Accountability is more than a buzzword. It's heard more and more in all sectors, especially lately with the exposure of high-profile scandals in the corporate, public, and not-for-profit sectors; if you're not paying attention, you may be held accountable for more than you anticipate.

Board members, private citizens, boards of trade, shareholders, and stakeholders—all are calling for governance reforms, including regular mandatory board evaluations—and so are activist groups.

Once strictly optional, board evaluations are now mandatory in certain sectors. While countless boards have evaluation policies in place, this does not mean that the policies are followed.

My recommendation is that you develop evaluation procedures, regardless of whether it's optional or mandatory in your area; follow through for your own protection, future, and reputation.

In the private sector, as potential investors become more educated and informed, board evaluation is becoming a vital factor when rating companies and determining their viability. This is great news for shareholders, as these practices are designed to improve the return on investment. Shareholders, too, benefit from increased transparency. Boards will no longer be able to hide behind a curtain of secrecy.

WHY YOU MAY NOT

Board evaluations will not happen if the directors themselves do not want to have their practices scrutinized. That begs the question, "Why wouldn't they?" My research has shown any number of reasons, but these are the top six:

- We do not mind evaluating the CEO, but members do not believe we should be evaluated.

- Who knows more about our board than we do? Therefore, who is capable of fulfilling the evaluation role?

- We are here because we were elected or appointed; therefore, we do not need to be evaluated.

- We can't afford to pay someone to carry out the evaluation.

- We have too much on our agendas and cannot take up board time with non-essential items.

- We are an excellent team; therefore, there is no reason to evaluate the board.

PROVING YOUR WORTH

More and more often, boards are being challenged to prove value and put themselves on a course of constant improvement and growth. Why should funds be used to support boards if they do not add value? Why should members/owners, who are facing less value for their hard-earned money, pay to bring a board together if the board is not representing them well and garnering benefits? Why would the public support not-for-profit boards if their donations are being used to finance board efforts, but there are no measurable results? Such questions may induce concern in even the most confident board members.

FEARS ASSOCIATED WITH EVALUATION

The concept of evaluation may raise real fears:

- I would be embarrassed if it is shown that the board is not adding value to this entity.

- What if someone finds out that we are spending too much time on items that are not within our sphere of control?

- What if we are not sticking to our mandate?

- What will others think if they discover that we are not a team and dysfunction is exposed?

- I am still on a learning curve, and I would not want others to see that I am not as competent in an area of governance as they think I should be.

- I am afraid that others will see that I am not as versed in the area of governance as they think I am.

When fears arise, it is easy for boards to rationalize why they avoid evaluations or why they engage in only minimal performance reviews.

MOTIVATIONS FOR EVALUATION

The type of evaluation is greatly determined by the motivation behind the evaluation. Not surprisingly, the type of evaluation selected affects the result obtained.

If the evaluation is conducted simply as a means to satisfy a requirement, it is inevitable that the bare minimum will be done and little, if any, improvement is likely to be visible. In such cases, the more common practice is to distribute a simple self-evaluation. In these situations, the board members may rate themselves in general terms and outstanding ratings are likely to be found. Unfortunately, these outstanding results are rarely based on any reliable evidence or the actual track record of the current board.

It is possible to move away from standard and generic evaluation tactics with current board-evaluation practices. Forward-looking boards can set out to add value through carefully planned and executed comprehensive evaluations. The process brings positive results for the board itself, the entity as a whole and, subsequently, for the shareholders and stakeholders. If a board is going to engage in an evaluation, it is just as well to do it right and reap the maximum benefits of the process. Often, this means engaging an external consultant.

PROFIT FROM THE PROFESSIONALS

Since many boards are ill equipped to take on the challenge of board evaluation internally, they look to outsiders. This is sound business practice. External consultants are neutral. Professional companies understand the process and are well aware of the best ways to tackle the project.

Companies who make this their business bring the wealth of knowledge and experience to the undertaking, and understand that each board is unique, requiring specific tailoring based on its culture, strategic directions, mandate, and goals. Yet—because there is nothing new under the sun—they may well have seen the issues or problems that may plague your board on other assignments.

Standardized or generic evaluation will not produce the quality results that need to be implemented to bring about real change and improvement. So, while external evaluation is the best option, this may be why there will always be boards unwilling, even if they have the time and money, to engage an external consultant.

SELF-EVALUATION IS THE REALITY

Each board has its strengths and weaknesses. Familiarization with the entity as a whole is critical to a comprehensive evaluation. There are bound to be issues with self-evaluation, and there are good reasons for that reality. With self-evaluation, board members may not truly recognize or be able to differentiate practices that are beneficial from those that are causing harm to the functionality of the board, thus preventing the board from achieving its mandate. Often, board members are unaware of the difference between governance and management. As a result, they may not have a clear picture of what is expected of them.

It is possible that a board may have been functioning inefficiently for years. As a result, it may not recognize what good governance and value-added look like. It is human nature to become complacent and comfortable with the status quo. This very notion is reason enough for setting standards and timelines for board evaluations. Evaluations serve as a perfect way to ignite board members' enthusiasm and increase interest in self-improvement in the area of governance. This interest is maintained, however, only when the motives behind the evaluation are honorable.

DESTRUCTIVE MOTIVES

Avoid using the results of an evaluation to clean house or remove members in a back-door fashion. If there is evidence of an ulterior motive, the evaluation is very likely to be ill received and board members will resent it.

Alternatively, when evaluations are endorsed the purpose is clear and legitimate with the intention to positively rejuvenate or re-energize the board. This is not to say that the results of the evaluation could not indicate that changes need to be made.

DO NOT RELY ON THE RESULTS OF AN EVALUATION TO CLEAN HOUSE

If changes are required, the board has an opportunity to put a legitimate process in place to ensure board members are treated with dignity and past work is respected. The board members would not be left feeling that the real intent was to 'get' somebody.

ACTIVE ENGAGEMENT—KEY TO SUCCESSFUL EVALUATION

Whether evaluations are internal or external, little can be accomplished with self-surveys or ready-made evaluation forms. The key to success is active and enthusiastic engagement by board members during the process. Once co-operation is established, the remaining task is to develop an appropriate evaluation process, keeping in mind that the most significant question is what to evaluate. The second consideration is how useful the results of the evaluation will prove to be for the board. This means that it's essential that the consultant understands the board's mandate, strategic directions, goals, and objectives.

FOCUSING ON CLEAR CONCISE GOALS

Evaluators must determine the *evaluation* goal of the company, organization, association, or council and identify the best way to achieve it. The evaluation is less likely to be successful in creating any real or beneficial improvements if it is not properly focused.

It is essential that questions are relevant to the accomplishment of the mandate and goals of the board, based on the needs of the board at the present time. Questions focus on improving board performance and are not designed to review all aspects of the organization. Board evaluations are, by their very nature, beneficial to any board. When they are properly conducted, they are invaluable.

THE PROCESS

The evaluation preparation process typically begins with dialogue, interviews, and a general discussion with a committee, the chairman, and select board members, or with the full board. Often, ways to improve the board function are discovered immediately. These discoveries, such as better time management during business meetings, can be acted upon immediately.

FOCUS ON ITEMS WITHIN THE BOARD'S SPHERE OF CONTROL TO USE TIME EFFICIENTLY

Many times these initial discussions show that board meetings are often full of interesting, yet not really relevant, conversations and discussions.

By simply focusing on items within the board's sphere of control, time is more efficiently used to the benefit of management, shareholders, and stakeholders.

When developing an evaluation plan, time management is only one of many areas on which a consultant would focus. There are diverse ways that a board evaluation can be developed and implemented. The consultant may prepare a survey, carefully tailored to the board, or choose to conduct interviews—or a group evaluation. This appeals to forward-thinking boards with directors who feel free to speak candidly with one another in an open forum.

DEALING WITH THE RESULTS

Board evaluations can achieve the following:

- Reveal issues that impede board improvement

- Help organizational advancement

- Bring focus back to the board room

- Help guide board members towards improvement, both individually and collectively, and

- Identify and solidify the appropriate roles and responsibilities of the board collectively.

When the results are known, it is essential for the board to ensure all members are actively engaged in the dialogue and understand the areas needing improvement.

Then it is important for the board to prepare a plan of action, assign responsibilities, and set timelines for follow-up to determine if the results being achieved match expectations and are desirable.

SET TIMELINES TO FOLLOW-UP THE RESULTS BEING ACHIEVED

MAINTAINING GOVERNANCE EXCELLENCE

It is vital for boards to complete evaluations regularly, follow-up on a scheduled basis, acknowledge progress, and give persons or teams credit for their achievements. We all know of boards that are not focused on improvement and remain reluctant and resistant to change.

The reality of these organizations tells the tale. However, boards seeking excellence and improvement in every way also exist and this should be the goal.

Such boards and organizations are continually evolving and implementing strategies designed to keep them functioning at an exceptional level. These boards are notable because they do not wait for externally-driven policies to come into effect to motivate or engage in evaluations. These boards expect excellence from others and require it from themselves.

Board evaluations are seen for what they are—tools for good governance.

7—KEEP BOARD MEMBERS HAPPY
IT'S GOOD GOVERNANCE…

THE BOARD AND HUMAN RESOURCES

Each board member is unique and brings value and one-of-a-kind knowledge and talent to the boardroom.

Although the ideal board hopes its members will be authentic—free to be transparent and say what they believe—without looking over their shoulders to see if they fit in or are accepted, this may not be the actuality.

The expectation is not that they *will go along to get along*. There is no room for *groupthink* in a great boardroom.

While most boards aim for this freedom, it may not always translate. The reason is likely ingrained in members' automatic responses.

Past influences the present. We make judgements continuously, often without analyzing why.

There may be risk in being authentic. To be true to themselves may require thoughtful action and going beyond the first, automatic response—and, perhaps, a little armchair therapy.

WE MAKE JUDGEMENTS WITHOUT ANALYZING WHY.

THERE IS RISK IN BEING AUTHENTIC

PAST INFLUENCES THE PRESENT

Growing up is a learning curve. We absorb the notion that we must behave in a certain way to be valued, accepted, included, and appreciated. Some are encouraged to be true to themselves—others learn that it is not acceptable to be their true selves and learn to deny who they are and behave as others expect.

Individuals may react with anger and frustration in certain surroundings or circumstances—neither is healthy. The boardroom needs to be a safe space for members to express themselves without fear of rejection or isolation.

JUDGEMENT WITHOUT ANALYZING

Many people like it best when everything is going smoothly. They do not want to deal with disagreements and conflict. They do not perceive differences of opinion as being healthy and acceptable. These people are judgemental and tend to make comments such as—

- Can you believe what he said?
- Who supported that, anyway?
- Did you vote against that motion?
- He is so difficult.
- I'm glad he's not here today; meetings run more smoothly when he isn't here.
- You knew he wouldn't vote for it if the rest of us did.

Know that people in general, including directors, do not want to hear differences of opinion if they make statements like—

- We always agree.
- We all seem to come to the same conclusions.
- All of our meetings run smoothly.
- We can almost read each other's minds.
- We never have any major disagreements.

Individuals must take an emotional risk if they find themselves in such environments.

THE RISK OF BEING AUTHENTIC

However grown up we might be, we can all feel rejected, put down, or isolated from the group. When board members are expected to comply, against their better judgement, this means their boards are asking that they reject who they really are in favor of pleasing fellow board members—this creates conditions ripe for *groupthink.*

It's not possible that every member will like what the others have to say 100 percent of the time. It is impossible to always appreciate different viewpoints on specific issues. When board members take the risk to speak their minds, they may feel exposed and vulnerable. Yet transparency and accountability are what make a great board.

Excellent boards that thrive want members to be authentic. These boards encourage directors to feel safe and be themselves by accepting them for who they are.

The best boards know that it is possible to be successful and unhappy at the same time. Therefore, they set the stage to ensure this is not the case. They want their members to feel fulfilled and know that they are leaving a positive legacy for the future.

ACTIONS TO ENSURE MEMBERS ARE TRUE TO THEMSELVES

Sometimes, board members may come to the realization that they are not finding board work very rewarding. Asking why may lead to assessment, a little armchair therapy, and result in decisions or actions such as the following:

- Accepting oneself

- Being inwardly content

- Being open

- Deciding what is best

- Putting their own opinion first

- Setting limits
- Speaking their truth
- Taking risks, and
- Taking stock.

ACCEPTING ONESELF

When directors realize they are not happy on their boards, they often stop and question why. They may recognize, as a first step, the need to accept themselves unconditionally.

When they can do this, they tend to approach their roles with new energy and an improved level of confidence.

They stop judging themselves harshly. They are not afraid of the criticism of others and begin to give constructive feedback in return. They do not need to be aggressive to make their views heard.

DIRECTORS MAY CHANGE HOW THEY APPROACH RESPONSIBILITIES BECAUSE THEY ACCEPT THEIR OWN TRUTHS

They are comfortable with themselves and accept the risks that are associated with the task of governance.

They may change how they approach their responsibilities, because they have been able to be introspective and accept their own truths. They are free to be themselves.

BEING INWARDLY CONTENT

Ideal board members come to realize that they may have all the accomplishments, wealth, and power in the world, but their most important achievement is to feel content.

They realize that their real worth comes from within. They do not need to fit in every situation, refrain from authenticity to be accepted, or to prove anything to anybody.

They have talents that are worthwhile and feel free to express them with confidence. If others do not accept those talents, that is their issue.

BEING OPEN

Being open leads to vulnerability. Open board members no longer hide who they really are to feel safe in the boardroom.

When they are open, they are transparent—the same on the outside as they are on the inside. They do not have to apologize for who they are or how they think.

Being open demonstrates inner strength. They realize that the best thing to do is to show who they are, thereby allowing others to be true to themselves. They refuse to second guess or judge others.

DECIDING WHAT IS BEST

When board members make the choice to be true to themselves, it can mean one of several things for the board.
They may—

- Appear to have changed

- Not be as compliant on certain issues as they were in the past

- Require more information before voting on specific issues

- Openly question certain board practices

- Expose dynamics that they feel are hurting the effectiveness of the board, or

- Leave the board.

They set new parameters on their commitments and relationships. They are willing to stop 'playing the game' if they determine it is not in their best interests or in the best interest of those they represent.

BEING OPINIONATED

Board members come to realize that every time they change or modify what they think in order to please others—they are not being authentic. They trust the fact that it is impossible to please everyone all of the time.

The key is that they care about others by listening openly, weighing everything they hear and read, and expressing their opinions freely.

SETTING LIMITS

Feeling used or under-appreciated is not what anyone wants to experience. Therefore, board members may begin to set limits. They may state the following:

- What they can and cannot do

- When they can and cannot meet

- What fits into their lifestyle and what does not

- Whether they work best on their own, in a small group, or in a large group, or

- What their talents are and the associated limits.

It becomes clear to the other board members that certain expectations and duties are acceptable and unacceptable. Thus, when they say 'no,' it really means no. When they say 'yes,' it means that they will accept the responsibility and be accountable for the results.

CERTAIN EXPECTATIONS AND DUTIES ARE ACCEPTABLE AND UNACCEPTABLE

SPEAKING THEIR TRUTH

Instead of feeling that they must agree with everything, board members begin to question what they truly think and express their opinions openly. They accept that their non-verbal behavior and tone of voice communicates volumes.

As a result, they find their truth and express it. They are no longer concerned about the repercussions they might face from the other directors.

They are confident that they are able to let others speak their truths without retaliation or without feeling defensive. They believe there is room for all opinions.

TAKING RISKS

Board members take real risks when they are willing to change the rules in areas that don't work as they envisage. They know what is satisfying and what no longer works. Therefore, they take chances and make choices that communicate the message, *'you may or may not like this, but this is the way it is going to be from here on in.'* They are no longer going to wait for others' approval to act.

The result is that their behavior might change and they object to things that they appeared to agree with in the past. That can be unsettling for the other board members.

The changing individual recognizes that others may not like the shifts and they are prepared for any negativity. They accept it and they do not change course. Others are given the clear message that this is the way it will be henceforth.

TAKING STOCK

When members examine the cost of being untrue to themselves in order to fit into the board, they may decide that the price is too high.

They may step back and re-evaluate why they have been willing to sacrifice who they truly are in order to remain on the board.

They will note how they fit and do not fit with their current groups. It is essential that they do not judge the other members, but focus on themselves and their reasons for being involved. They discover who they are, what they believe, and acknowledge their values.

CORPORATE CULTURE

Successful organizations have strong cultures. Strong cultures begin with authentic behavior, exhibited when people know to express their opinions openly without being attacked or rejected. In organizations, this begins in the boardrooms. People trust that they do not have to dress like everyone else, speak like everyone else, or clone themselves in any way.

Diversity is honored. In return, individuals know that their voices are heard and they are able to support the decisions of their boards. They do not have to 'get their way' all the time. They are seen, heard, and their input and work is valued.

8—WHO HAS THE POWER? BOARD CHAIR OR CEO?

MANAGING THE BOARD

Frequent self-evaluation, which I recommend as an important step in practical governance between formal evaluations, shows who really runs the board. Often, when board members change frequently, the most influential person is the CEO. This chapter addresses how this happens, and how the board can assume its proper role.

HOW A BOARD LOSES CONTROL

This occurs when the board

- Relies too heavily on the CEO for information

- Does not do its homework by reading materials and connecting with stakeholders

- Decides that friendship is more important than governance

- Condones covert manipulation

- Does not clarify its mandate

- Knows board member are there for the wrong reasons, but ignores their behavior

- Does not evaluate risks

- Fails to assume the governance role

- Fails to prioritize agenda items, or

- There is no plan.

While reading, identify whether any of these practices exist in your board and determine what you can do to regain governance control.

THE BOARD RELIES TOO HEAVILY ON THE CEO FOR INFORMATION

Board members wear many hats. These include representing themselves as individuals and representing the following:

- A specific group, if nominated by a group

- Individuals who are marginalized

- Users of the organization's programs and services

- Consumers

- The legal and/or moral owners, or

- Partners key to the specific entity's success.

When any topic comes before the board, it is essential for the members to consider the matter from all perspectives, knowing the relevant factors related to each of the perspectives, and evaluating all of the associated risks.

In cases where a board relies solely on the CEO, members may be assuming that the CEO is considering issues and the risks from all perspectives. This may not be the case if the CEO is determined on the board's consent without too much discussion. Once the decision is made, it's too late to say *we would have done things differently if we had known these facts*. It is the directors' responsibility to stay informed and be aware of the facts.

The board must take responsibility to look at each issue from every angle and rely on the CEO only as a single information source.

DOES THE BOARD KNOW HOW TO DO ITS HOMEWORK?

Board members are busy people. When a board does not advise potential members of the full nature of the commitment, they are not prepared that it takes more than brushing up on background materials to connect with stakeholders. The work may include regularly scheduled board meetings, special meetings, committee meetings, and stakeholder consultations, just to name a few—plus the obligation to connect with stakeholders.

When board members attend without having read the materials, it slows progress and discussion. If this occurs, boards should evaluate whether the reference or resource information provided is too long or complex or not strictly relevant to the topic at hand. Present the information in a simple, easy to absorb form, such as a one or two page briefing note:

- On each topic

- Relevant background details in point form

- The issue at hand

- Options for the board to consider

- Pros and cons (risks) associated with each option, and

- Potential political fallout (public or media).

When the information is comprehensive and easy to read, the members are in a position to compare it with what they hear from their stakeholders.

There is an assumption that the board has identified its key stakeholders and that all members are in agreement. Each group of relevant stakeholders may have a different opinion about a topic, and all opinions may well be expressed at the board table prior to any decision.

THE BOARD DECIDES THAT FRIENDSHIP IS MORE IMPORTANT THAN GOVERNANCE

Friendship becomes more important than open discussion and divergent opinions in certain circumstances:

- When the board operates in a small geographical area
- If board members are interdependent in other areas of their life
- Individuals sit on the board because it is the thing to do
- There is a lack of commitment to achieving the mandate
- It is the line of least resistance and, therefore, maintains harmony
- Everyone feels comfortable with the system
- The CEO's methods are autocratic
- Board members feel they are incompetent compared to the CEO
- Board members are made to feel guilty if they do not 'trust' the CEO
- The personal benefits of accepting everything the CEO puts forth outweigh the negatives, or
- 'Groupthink' is the norm during board meetings.

Open and honest discussion where divergent opinions exist is essential to effective governance. It is important to value the input of the CEO. However, it is also vital to consider all data, information, and risks prior to making any decision.

THE BOARD CONDONES COVERT MANIPULATION

Many forms of covert manipulation may occur:

- A chosen few make the decision prior to the board meeting and inform others of the 'right' choice before the discussion begins
- A board member contacts fellow members to garner support prior to bringing an issue to the board table
- Tabling an item when the people who would object to the decision are not present

- Bargaining with other board members and agreeing to vote with them on their issue if they support this issue, and

- The CEO and board chair decide and take action prior to the board meeting and inform the board at the meeting, knowing that it would be too late to change the course at that time.

It is possible to identify when such circumstances occur and follow a problem-solving process to eliminate them.

THE BOARD DOES NOT CLARIFY ITS MANDATE

A board exists for a specific reason. If too many factions are represented, the mandate can become so broad that productive action is rare. Each board leaves a positive legacy when it focuses solely on its mandate. To leave such a legacy, it is critical for the board to review the mandate frequently and question whether or not its actions are designed for achievement.

It is too easy to expand a mandate or change directions, swayed by the opinions of influential board members. It is equally easy to leave the organization with programs and services it cannot fund because the risks were not evaluated.

Risks may include the inability to: hire knowledgeable personnel on a permanent basis, maintain the equipment or materials purchased via special funding or grants, continue to fund the program or service without taking resources from other programs or services. One political risk is creating friction with other entities if they perceive the board as encroaching on what has been traditionally been their area. Another risk is created when boards are obliged to scale back services they once offered.

THE BOARD KNOWS THAT CERTAIN MEMBERS ARE THERE FOR THE WRONG REASONS, YET IGNORES THEIR BEHAVIOR

When directors join the board for the wrong reasons, their disinterest influences its effectiveness and, by default, affects the CEO. When the board is divided and dysfunctional, the CEO has no choice but to step in and use his influence. He does this to ensure key decisions are made in a timely manner, ensuring the entity does not lose its credibility or momentum.

The chair can only build a strong effective team when he has the cooperation of members. When he does not have the skills to build the team, a consultant will assist to reach that goal.

THE BOARD DOES NOT EVALUATE RISKS

In one situation, a choice or event may pose a risk. In another, it may not. The Decision Making Model of Governance poses a definite view of the decision making process to avoid or minimize risks.

THE PROCESS

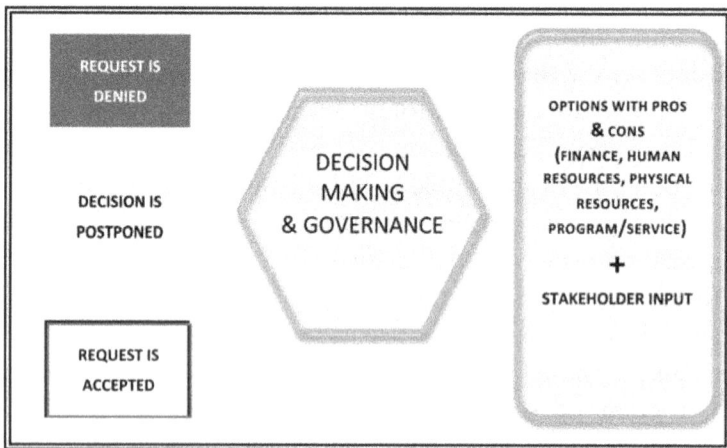

If the board does not govern risks, the CEO has no other choice but to try and do it alone. If she does not avoid risks and the entity faces serious consequences, the board may use the CEO as a scapegoat, blaming her for inefficiencies. Rarely would a CEO want to engage in tasks focused on dealing with negative fallout, especially if it could have been avoided. The CEO is aware that her time would be better spent focusing on the mandate, demonstrating success, maintaining harmony, and the positive image of the entity.

It is important to acknowledge that not all risks can be eliminated or avoided. There are necessary risks each board has to take, especially when it is dealing with conflicting demands from multiple stakeholders.

THE BOARD FAILS TO ASSUME THE GOVERNANCE ROLE

Governance is equivalent to oversight. It is not management. When it is trying to determine whether a task is one or the other, a board should ask, "What components of this issue require only the board's attention, and which components fall clearly within the role the board assigned to the CEO?" If that question fails, ask, "Why couldn't we trust the CEO to deal with this issue?"

The CEO is more likely to assume governance responsibilities when he is concerned or when experience has taught him that, if he brings the issue to the board, it will meddle in management and increase his ineffectiveness.

THE BOARD FAILS TO PRIORITIZE AGENDA ITEMS

Prior to tackling any agenda, it is imperative for board members to identify the purpose of each item. As indicated, divide items into Decision, Information, and Advice.

Information items are there to provide updates and material about areas of interest to board members. Since these items hold the lowest priority on the agenda ladder, they can be provided in bullet or report form to be read at leisure when the meeting schedule does not allow time for review.

Since *advice* items are topics on the agenda to obtain the opinion of the board or members, it stands to reason that the seeker does not have to take the board's advice. He may be seeking multiple opinions and the board's opinion is only one. These, like the *information* items, would not displace *decision* items.

Decision items always hold the highest priority placement. A meeting would not end with decisions left unmade because too much time was devoted to information or advice items. Making governance decisions is the board's role and it cannot be abdicated for any reason. When a board fails to fulfill its role, the CEO has to continue to manage the organization and may be forced to make decisions that could be better made by the board.

THERE IS NO PLAN

In the absence of a definite plan, somebody has to make decisions to focus the efforts of the organization. That person will be the CEO. He knows that he has limited resources and it is essential that he be viewed as transparent, fair, accountable, and organized. He is required to use good judgement to protect the organization and meet the expectations of the users/consumers. There has to be substance. If there is only form, the entity will begin to flounder under his leadership.

To keep the entity on a sure footing, the board can develop a plan that's realistic, achievable, and measureable. The board will retain ownership of the plan and monitor progress on a regular basis. The board is the champion of the plan, and the CEO knows that the board is holding him accountable for this contribution to its achievement. The board holds itself accountable for the goals and objectives that are entirely within its purview.

DEVELOP A PLAN THAT'S REALISTIC, ACHIEVABLE, AND MEASURABLE.

A board will avoid all of these issues by accepting and fulfilling its role.

FIVE WAYS TO ASSUME THE BOARD ROLE

Boards play a vital role in democratic societies. There are five key actions boards can take to ensure that governance is separated from management:

- Adopt transparent and accountable practices
- Define how its role is different from the role of the CEO
- Define its standards of practice
- Demonstrate leadership qualities, and
- Govern risks.

ADOPT TRANSPARENT AND ACCOUNTABLE PRACTICES

It is possible for a board to establish practices for each component of its role:

- Outline how it establishes its agenda

- Determine, in advance, when and where it will hold its regularly scheduled meetings

- Communicate with stakeholders when meetings are open and when they are closed

- Seek divergent opinions and encouraging openness

- Adopt a conflict resolution process

- Ensure all board members are free to speak their opinions without any repercussions

- Evaluate the effectiveness of board meetings

- Evaluate the effectiveness of the board and the board members, as well as the CEO

- Monitor its progress

- Accept the role it has in the entity's success and its failures

- Admit when it made an error in judgement

- Work in harmony with partners

- Work with a 'win-win' philosophy at all times, and

- Make governance decisions only.

THE BOARD DEFINES HOW ITS ROLE IS DIFFERENT FROM THE ROLE OF THE CEO

It is not difficult to write a role description for the board and one for the CEO. Separate the roles and identify any overlaps that could cause conflict in the future.

During this process, it is essential to determine if the board could meet without the CEO present, and the circumstances that would need to exist for the board to make that choice.

THE BOARD DEFINES ITS STANDARDS OF PRACTICE

These standards are written in governance policies and include the code of ethics for the board. There is no need to explain why a policy is a policy. There is a need to ensure the policy is realistic, can be implemented, and measured.

The board never loses focus on the idea that it's the people that make the organization and the board, and not the policies or the things that it owns. Everyone needs to be aware of the consequences of non-compliance with the policies and standards.

THE BOARD DEMONSTRATES LEADERSHIP QUALITIES

Ask this question, "Do we have any items on our agenda that have been there for months?" If the answer is 'yes,' it may be time to revisit the board's decision making process. Effective boards know when they need to make decisions and they do everything in their power to fulfill this role.

They do not procrastinate or look to others to resolve issues. They are proactive and demonstrate strong leadership qualities.

THE BOARD GOVERNS RISKS

Very few boards have the privilege of working in an unchanging environment. Those that practice excellence in governance accept divergent stances and negotiate settlements among conflicting views. The board does not avoid risks; it mitigates risks in order to achieve the goals and objectives in its plan. It knows its values and does not violate them. The board accepts responsibility for its actions. It learns from its mistakes and encourages the CEO to do the same.

The board expects excellence and sets a tone of harmony and cooperation. It expresses appreciation to the CEO and to its partnership and acknowledges their contributions to its success.

9—HOLDING THE CEO ACCOUNTABLE

BOARDS AND MANAGEMENT

Boards are accountable. However, board members are not present every day and are unable to control everything the CEO does on a daily basis. Mechanisms are required to enable the board to determine whether the CEO is ensuring that the organization operates effectively and efficiently within applicable policies and legislation, and is cognizant of external factors that could influence the longitudinal well-being of the entity.

There are at least eight actions a board can take to hold the CEO responsible for the management of the organization:

- Governance planning
- Focus on vision
- Risk oversight
- Reporting schedule
- Knowing what is expected and when
- Trends
- Hiring practices, and
- CEO focus.

GOVERNANCE PLANNING

It is essential that a board's governance plan is separate from the management plan.

The governance plan contains the mission, goals, and objectives. The CEO supports the implementation of the governance plan and also establishes priorities to be accomplished within the organization.

THE GOVERNANCE PLAN CONTAINS THE MISSION, GOALS, AND OBJECTIVES.

Making these priorities explicit is important for the management team. An example of such a priority could relate to professional development required to meet changing industry standards or organizational needs. There may be many needs, but the CEO and her team have to decide what can be supported from risk, financial, and human resource perspectives.

The similarity in both plans is that the goals are time-limited, clear, concise, achievable, and measurable.

FOCUS ON VISION

The board establishes a vision for a reason. Therefore, it is vital to see evidence that the CEO is focused on that vision and refraining from implementing her own vision, particularly if it is different from the board's.

It is also essential to question how major decisions are supporting the attainment of that vision and how it is being communicated to key stakeholders and partners.

RISK OVERSIGHT

Often boards complain they do not know how to find the balance between oversight and micromanagement. One method is to use a risk checklist.

This ensures that the board can be aware of essential operational details, without being involved with them. This checklist also delineates areas of worry for the board and may vary from board to board.

Here is an example of one board's checklist:

- Deductions have been remitted on their due dates (for example, Workers' Compensation premiums, payroll deductions, pension contributions, dues, such as union or professional, health premiums, payroll tax, and business or related tax premiums)

- There are no known instances of contravention of any applicable laws that could create a liability, no legal claim outstanding against the board, and, where there is an outstanding claim—the board has full details

- Board of director insurance is in place, and

- Financial reports are filed as required.

This checklist would be signed by the CEO and other applicable personnel before being submitted to the board at designated intervals.

REPORTING SCHEDULE

There are many topics of interest competing for the board's attention. Unfortunately, many of these topics can be addressed comprehensively only at certain times of the year. Therefore, it is essential for the board to identify, with the CEO, when accurate meaningful information can be reported. The result of such discussion should be a schedule of topics that the CEO will address at specified meetings.

If the CEO is unable to present the required data, she would provide an explanation and the date when the information shall be made available.

KNOWING WHAT'S EXPECTED AND WHEN

How often the CEO reports to the board will depend on the frequency of board meetings and the amount of time that can be devoted to the CEO report, which should address the following:

- The objectives in the strategic plan

- Issues that are political and/or publicly sensitive

- Outstanding accomplishments or challenges that the organization is facing, and

- Topics agreed upon by the board and CEO.

It is unreasonable for a board to expect a report on every program, service, or product. If the board creates such an expectation, it will receive volumes of material, much of which will be imprecise and lack substance, even if it appears impressive.

TO SAVE TIME, DIRECTORS SHOULD RECEIVE THE CEO'S REPORT IN ADVANCE

The CEO may be (should be…) very busy. Time spent writing vague information or creating fillers in order to impress the board is time the CEO cannot spend focusing on the effectiveness and efficiency of the organization.

To save time in meetings, it is possible to request that directors receive the CEO's report in advance. Then it is only necessary for the CEO to speak to critical points and answer questions.

TRENDS

Whether the board oversees a business, a union, a not-for-profit, an association, or a public-sector organization, it is still essential to be aware of trends and their impact on important areas:

- Sales

- Standards

- Job security

- Extraneous costs such as taxes

- The sustainability of programs, services, and products

- What people want or expect, and

- Availability of human resources and recruitment methods.

Recognizing that board work is only one part of a director's busy life, how does a board keep on top of trends?

One solution is to look to the CEO. The CEO is the conduit between society at large and the board. She is the person who is expected to read, engage in discussions with others, and network to comprehend the trends that will influence the organization in the near and distant future.

Another way is to ask each board member to monitor specific trends or sectors.

HIRING PRACTICES

The success of any organization is often dependent on the talents and skills of the management team. Since the CEO hires her team, it is essential for the board to note whether or not the CEO hires a strong one.

If she does, the board can usually rest assured that the entity is in good hands. If she does not hire a competent team with excellent team building, conflict resolution, and managerial skills, the body may be at risk.

These risks can relate to the reputation, the financial health, the stability, or the ability of the organization to cope with change and sustain itself well into the future.

Any hiring decisions based on nepotism, fear, or personal needs can hurt the entity and should be of concern to any board of directors.

CEO FOCUS

It is essential for the CEO to keep her focus on the customer/client/user. She is the person who would meet with these groups and articulate their needs, challenges, frustrations, and goals.

If the CEO becomes focused on self-promotion, her own benefits, or her own future directions, she is unable to gain the information needed to ensure the organization is attentive to its vision and mandate.

She may ask the directors to make decisions that are not in the entity's best interests and can negatively affect the board's reputation.

Boards can no longer avoid oversight. They are no longer simply functional as window dressing for organizations. Boards are accountable for the well-being of their organizations. Thus, it is incumbent upon them to find ways to hold their CEOs accountable.

10—HOW TO KEEP YOUR BOARD ON TRACK

CONTROLLING INFLUENCES ON THE BOARD

Stakeholders and shareholders do influence boards. This influence may be positive and supportive or destructive and debilitating. This chapter focuses on five common ways stakeholders and shareholders inhibit board work and outlines strategies boards can use to deal with such situations.

The first issue is interference in, and derailment of, the board's decision making process. The second is placing pressure on board members and causing decision paralysis. The third and fourth relate to blaming the board for lack of consultation or causing the board to ignore its own policies. The final topic is failure to follow through on commitments.

INTERFERENCE

You may have noticed that stakeholders rarely take an interest in board activities until there is something they dislike or some action they want taken. That can be frustrating. However, it is essential for boards to be aware if this is a familiar pattern and prepare for it.

How would the board do this? By asking a series of questions and making sure it has articulated how to respond. Here are some questions and solutions for ways boards can be diligent to circumvent interference issues.

QUESTION—WHEN DO STAKEHOLDERS BEGIN TO ENGAGE WITH THE BOARD?

Solution

- Name the issues.

QUESTION—HOW DOES THE BOARD PREPARE FOR STAKEHOLDER ENGAGEMENTS?

Solutions

- Realize who outlines the key messages.

- Review (or write) the dispute resolution process the board uses.

- Analyze the communication process (step by step) used by the board currently. Determine its effectiveness and modify it as necessary.

- Ensure the board chair, members, and the CEO know their roles during any engagement.

- Understand the board's stakeholder consultation process. If one does not exist, establish one.

QUESTION—HOW MAY THE BOARD MAINTAIN A POSITIVE STANCE AT ALL TIMES?

Solutions

- Review the code of conduct expected of the board and CEO.

- Ensure meeting arrangements are conducive for the board and stakeholders.

- Provide sufficient notice of all meetings and consultations.

- Open clearly defined communication avenues.

- Ensure the board has a way to deal with a board member or the CEO if either does not follow the agreed process and/or procedures.

- Know or establish a reassessment process, which is used when a stakeholder presents a new concern or information requiring the board to reconsider an issue in a new light.

QUESTION—HOW DOES THE BOARD DEAL WITH FALSE OR INACCURATE INFORMATION PRESENTED TO STAKEHOLDERS?

Solutions

- Review the data gathering process used by the board.

- Know the risk-oversight process.

- Memorize the communication guidelines and honor them at all times.

- Prepare to admit when information is questionable or inaccurate and avoid cover-ups.

- Avoid defending past actions, which were based on inaccurate information, and agree to go back to the board table and gather or consider the new information.

The key to keeping the board on track is to ensure that stakeholder engagement does not lead to decision paralysis.

DECISION PARALYSIS

Some people are indecisive and will keep the board mired in considering an issue to the point where a decision is never made.

If your board is in this situation, you'll know. You'll likely face the following circumstances:

- Issues that remain on the agenda meeting after meeting.

- Members who complain that their issues are never discussed.

- Stakeholders who accuse the board of lack of consultation and communication about specific issues.

- Splinter groups formed within the board.

If you see these signs of decision paralysis, use the series questions yourself and with the board, and make sure you know what to do to avoid a recurrence of this type of paralysis in the future.

The following questions and actions are designed for boards to use as support during this process.

QUESTION—ARE THERE UNRESOLVED ISSUES THAT REMAIN ON THE AGENDA?

Solutions

- Set timelines (i.e., a board must deal with all issues within a six-month time period).

- Ensure there is a mechanism to bring all governance issues to the table and hold the CEO accountable for all management options.

- Ensure board members' issues are dealt with in a designated manner.

QUESTION—IS THE BOARD GIVEN TOO MANY CHOICES AND NOT GIVEN THE PROS AND CONS ASSOCIATED WITH EACH ISSUE?

Solutions

- Ensure the issue, the risks, and the options for each are clearly delineated.

- Eliminate options that are not within the board's sphere of control, within its mandate, or within its resource envelope.

- Discuss remaining options with the primary stakeholders to ensure the board has all the information it needs to make the decision.

- Make a decision and design a communication plan to implement it in concert with those who are going to agree with it and those who may object.

- Take action.

When boards do not act or consult key players, they are setting themselves up for negative consequences.

BLAMING THE BOARD

One of the easiest options for stakeholders when boards do not consult is to blame the board. Rather accept responsibility and engage in the process, often people want someone to blame when things do not go their way.

Avoid the blame game and the creation of more problems. Instead, use the proven method of asking a series of questions, thereby engaging others. This serves to remind them of the benefits of their involvement in the process.

The following questions and actions are designed to support the board's efforts.

QUESTION—DOES THE BOARD HAVE A CONSULTATION PROCESS?

Solutions

- Know the timeframes.

- Name participants.

- Let the board know if you think you should participate.

- Know who covers the costs.

- Note whether minutes are kept.

QUESTION—HOW OFTEN DOES IT HAPPEN?

Solutions

- Know the steps in the board's environmental scan (such as issues, impact, resources, outcomes, etc).

- Take note of the dates of each event.

QUESTION—HOW ARE ALL VOICES HEARD?

Solutions

- Note whether the forum is convenient for all interested stakeholders.

- Know whether participation is by choice or by invitation.

- Understand how you represent all of those you choose to represent without having to take sides.

QUESTION—ARE YOU FREE TO SPEAK ON BEHALF OF OTHERS?

Solutions

- Determine how various persons or groups think.

- Know how they differ from each other.

- Determine if people may be left out of the process.

- Assess how partners view the issue.

- Understand how you see things.

Consultation and communication are fundamental to the success of all great boards. Boards may face serious reprisals when they fail to consult.

NON-COMPLIANCE WITH CURRENT POLICIES

It is easy to get caught up in the emotion of individual stories when certain board members want something done. Make sure, in the doing, that any action is in line with current governance policies. Otherwise, follow the policy modification process.

Here, too, questions are the way forward and help ensure that the board is in compliance with current policies and that actions/resolutions are in place and outlined clearly. These questions ensure the board is exercising due diligence, instead of being swayed by emotion.

QUESTION—WHAT DOES THIS PERSON/GROUP WANT AND IS IT IN LINE WITH CURRENT POLICIES?

Solutions

- Know when policies were last reviewed.

- Know how to remove outdated policies.

- Remember that all decisions become policies.

- Remember that any action can set a precedent for future decisions.

- Follow due process when modifying existing policies.

QUESTION—HOW DOES THE BOARD DENY A REQUEST THAT IS NOT IN LINE WITH CURRENT POLICIES?

Solutions

- Understand how decisions are communicated to stakeholders (by whom, when, and how).

- Ensure the board has a board-approved appeals process.

- Note how the board resolves disputes.

QUESTION—HOW DOES THE BOARD PREVENT ACTIONS BY THE BOARD CHAIR OR THE BOARD EXECUTIVE THAT ARE NOT IN LINE WITH BOARD POLICIES?

Solutions

- Note how board members are expected to uphold the board policies and the sanctions if they do not (i.e., never overspend, never provide personal loans to the CEO, or never make unsanctioned payments).

- If a policy committee exists, support its efforts.

- Understand how the board checks its policies prior to taking a vote on a motion.

Action or inaction by the board can make or break its reputation. Therefore, it is critical for a board to honor its policies, follow established processes, and keep its commitments.

KEEPING COMMITMENTS

Boards have the dual responsibility of fulfilling not only their own commitments, but of honoring any obligations made by the previous board(s). It is not helpful when new directors ignore the agreements made by previous boards or before they joined. Understanding your obligations is essential. Ask questions and prepare diligently.

The following questions are excellent for board use as a whole and as a guide for individual members on procedure.

QUESTION—WHO ARE OUR PARTNERS, COMPETITORS, AND PRIMARY STAKEHOLDERS?

Solutions

- List the partners, competitors, and primary stakeholders.

- Know their key representatives.

- Be cognizant of when you meet with or interact with them.

- Know the objectives of the interactions.

- Be prepared to communicate the board's key messages.

QUESTION—WHO ARE OUR OWNERS?

Solutions

- Know the legal owners.

- Understand their expectations.

- Note how the board keeps its commitments to the legal owners.

- Know how the board demonstrates that it is accountable.

QUESTION—WHICH COMMITMENTS ARE THE BOARD OBLIGATED TO FULFILL?

Solutions

- Keep a list of these commitments.

- Keep a file with the board's action plans.

- Note when key decisions need to be made and support the board in those efforts.

- Understand how the board evaluates progress.

QUESTION—WHAT IS MY ROLE?

Solutions

- Know your role in each process.

- Live up to your obligations.

- Know others' roles and respect those roles.

Boards expect others to honor their obligations, thus it is essential for boards to keep their commitments to others.

FINAL COMMENT

Board work is challenging and rewarding. Disagreement is essential to progress and growth and certain stakeholder and shareholders are easier to deal with than others. Preventing stakeholders and shareholders from inhibiting the work of the board means being familiar with the strategies to deal with such situations that we focused on in this chapter.

Boards can be proactive and maintain a constructive stance during all interactions. Using the questions and actions presented here will support yours as you endeavor to fulfill your duty of governance.

11— ESSENTIAL NETWORKING SKILLS FOR BOARD MEMBERS

INTRODUCTION

Most board members realize it is important to connect with those they represent.

These connections can be made in many ways:

- Local chambers of commerce

- Involvement in non-profit organizations such as Rotary Clubs

- Participation in professional development activities sponsored by other entities

- Participation in board sponsored events, and

- Informal gatherings.

Irrespective of the type of event or situation, four critical questions need to be addressed:

- Does each board member need to possess specific skills in order to network effectively?

- Are there written or unwritten rules board members need to follow?

- Are there pitfalls board members need to avoid?

- Does the board need policies that address the area of representation?

This chapter addresses each of these questions.

SKILLS BOARD MEMBERS NEED IN ORDER TO NETWORK EFFECTIVELY

During a board member's tenure, he will have many opportunities to network with other directors, partners, shareholders, and stakeholders. To network effectively requires certain skills. Here are tips to the top 11:

> 1) Asking a question that requires more than a one-word answer

It is easier for the board member to initiate a fluid conversation when he is comfortable asking open-ended questions.

Open-ended questions are clear in their aim. They can elicit a range of responses and they do not require the respondent to try and figure out what the board member might want to hear.

> 2) Finishing the conversation

When a board member initiates a conversation, it is important that he pay attention to the other person and refrain from scanning the room.

Also, finish any conversation before rushing off to meet the next person. This act alone can be taken as insincerity and is unlikely to generate good will from the other participant in the conversation.

> 3) Identifying commonalities

A board member who is able to identify what she has in common with another individual is more likely to put the other person at ease and gain more information. The second person relaxes and may initiate conversation about the things they have in common. Then the board member can shift the conversation to a topic of interest to her, if that is her intent during this encounter.

4) Identifying with whom he needs to network

A board member has to be open to talking to everyone, but there may be certain people with whom he feels he needs to touch base during an event.

It will be vital for him to scan the room and spot those individuals. Then he can think about and be prepared for the times an opportunity might arise to make that contact. However, it's important not to be obvious about it.

5) Being thoroughly familiar with the board's issues

Each board member is responsible for understanding the topics that are relevant to his board. He knows what he has to keep confidential and the key messages that need to be communicated. He identifies any misinformation that is being presented to him and ascertains how he can resolve this situation. He does not pretend to be more knowledgeable than he is. Neither does he comment on issues that are in the management's domain.

6) Listening actively while going with the flow of the conversation

A board member who is an active listener is able to identify quickly when the other person is shifting the focus of the conversation. It is essential for the board member to follow that person's train of thought because there may be critical information that needs to come back to the board.

If the shift is about an irrelevant topic, then the board member can return the topic to his area of interest. Good conversations are a two-way process.

7) Scanning the crowd

Board members find themselves in many different contexts. It's essential to scan each room and identify individuals by some dominant characteristic. These could include their names, positions, home towns, or clubs. When someone is of interest but the board member does not know him, it's acceptable to ask someone he trusts to identify the person of interest, or to remind him of that person's name.

8) Observing what is noteworthy

One way to start a conversation is to note something that stands out. It may be a logo on a person's coat, briefcase, or folio. Taking note of someone specific can act as an ice breaker and provide the opportunity to start a conversation.

9) Planning

A good networking skill to hone is planning questions that one can ask when the conversation dies. To do this, the board member would think of the context and identify three or four questions to ask at a dead end when the dialogue is starting to feel awkward. These questions breathe new life into the conversation.

10) Remaining positive

As long as an individual is a board member, she is representing the board. Therefore, it is vital for her to remain positive, even in the face of adversity. Resistance creates resistance, thus the most successful networker listens carefully, takes the opinions of others under advisement, and refrains from contradicting others unnecessarily during networking sessions. She states the board's views in a positive manner.

11) Taking an interest in each person as an individual

When a person is out of his context, it is even more essential for a board member to focus on this person as an individual. Sometimes the person does not want to be always identified with his business, social group, or as part of an organization. He wants to be seen for who he is and he does not want the board member pigeon-holing him for any reason.

THE WRITTEN OR UNWRITTEN RULES BOARD MEMBERS ARE EXPECTED TO FOLLOW

When board members communicate with others in the network, it is essential that they know the board's written and unwritten rules. For example, an unwritten rule may be that board members communicate with other board members and stakeholders, while the board chairperson communicates with board chairpersons and other high ranking officials.

Whatever the rules, the director has a right to know them to avoid embarrassment or negative repercussions from the board.

PITFALLS TO AVOID

Each board member should avoid seven key pitfalls when networking:

- Commenting on the CEO's performance

- Divulging any confidential information

- Stating his own opinion when the policy of the board is that the board speaks with one voice

- Revealing the contents of discussions prior to the board making a decision

- Inciting others to bring issues to the board rather than handling the issue himself

- Negatively commenting on the behavior of another board member, and

- Criticizing a process designed and approved by the board.

THE BOARD'S POLICIES ON THE TOPIC OF REPRESENTATION

It is essential for board members to know when they can and cannot represent the board. Topics to consider include—

- Who is the official spokesperson for the board?

Board policy may be that the spokesperson for the board is the board chairperson in all situations.

- What can a board member communicate to another organization if he was appointed to this board by that organization?

A board member may be expected to convey pre-determined key messages to these organizations.

- When can a board member convey his own opinion to his constituents?

A board may not want a director sharing his own opinion at any time. The board member is expected to uphold and state the decisions of the collective only.

- When does the board speak on management issues?

The board may confine its role to speaking on governance issues only. The CEO may be expected to act as the spokesperson for management issues.

FINAL COMMENT

To avoid embarrassment and negative feedback from the board, each member has a right to receive professional development on networking, unwritten and written rules, and the governance representation policies.

12— WHO SHOULD DEVELOP THE BOARD'S AGENDA?

INTRODUCTION

Who develops the agenda for your board meetings? When I ask this question, I am given one of the following answers:

- The CEO

- The board chair and the CEO

- The board's executive committee, or

- The board.

Invariably someone asks if it really makes a difference. I believe it does. This chapter examines the pros and cons associated with each approach to developing the agenda.

THE CEO DEVELOPS THE AGENDA

The CEO is an employee of the board and as such he has a very demanding role. His goal is to ensure the organization is managed well and the entity is focused on achieving its mandate. His focus is within the entity. This statement is not made to undermine the amount of time a CEO devotes to supporting the board as it completes its work. However, it does imply that the board needs a CEO who is dedicated to the management of the entity and one who respects the governance role of the board. What are the benefits and drawbacks of the CEO completing the agenda?

THE PROS
The CEO—

- Is aware of the pressing issues within the organization

- May possess a historical perspective of issues that new board members may not have at this point in time

- Will be aware of the items demanding his time as he completes his role

- Has access to the resources to complete the board packages, and

- May be more knowledgeable than the board members about the board's issues.

THE CONS
The CEO—

- May bring forth issues, which are within his sphere of control to resolve and engage the board in the management of the entity, thereby absolving him of his responsibility

- May provide large board information packages and expect the board members to absorb all of the details. Directors may not have the time to read the material thoroughly and require briefing notes to consolidate the issues, creating extra work, and

- May not understand the responsibilities associated with governance. As a result, the board may fail to complete its role effectively.

THE BOARD CHAIR AND THE CEO COMPLETE THE BOARD'S AGENDA

When the board chair partners with the CEO to complete the agenda, it is assumed that the board has grappled with the following questions and determined that this is the best approach.

- Who comprises the governance team?

- Is the chair of the board one member of the governance team or is he the boss of the board?

- Who is responsible for the governance of the entity—the board chair or the full board?

- Do the board members understand how to generate the board agenda in advance of board meetings?

- Do board members understand how to plan their year?

- Do the board members understand how to differentiate items that need decisions from those items that are provided for enlightenment or those that are asking for the board's advice?

Answering these questions takes time. They are neglected where boards begin with full agendas and fail to reflect on their role and how it is different from that of the CEO's.

THE PROS
The Board Chair and the CEO—

- Are aware of the pressing matters within the organization and the key governance issues

- May come up with new items that are demanding of the CEO's time and that place the board at risk

- Know the resources needed to complete the board packages and can require the staff to prepare packages as directed by the board's criteria, and

- May be more knowledgeable than the board members about the board's issues.

THE CONS

The Board Chair and the CEO may—

- Not have a thorough handle on the difference in their roles (As a result, the board chair may rely on the CEO and place management issues on the board's agenda, thus absolving the CEO of his responsibility.)

- Discuss many of the issues when preparing the agenda and fail to recognize that this automatically places the other board members at a disadvantage when they come to the board meeting

- Become a team and the board chair may not want to ask the CEO to provide briefing notes (that require staff resources) to accompany large amounts of data placed in board member packages

- Fail to differentiate the responsibilities associated with governance from those associated with the management of the entity

- Not recognize that the board chair is isolating himself from the board team and is being viewed as an advocate for the CEO, and

- Increase the possibility that the board will neglect its governance responsibilities and fail to discuss its governance role and plan its year.

THE EXECUTIVE COMMITTEE OF THE BOARD DESIGNS THE BOARD'S AGENDA

Many boards have an executive committee because—

- The board is large and the financial costs requires the board to streamline its processes.

- The board is unable to meet frequently.

- Time-limited or emergency decisions are required between board meetings and it is not possible to convene special meetings of the full board, or

- The board decided this is the best way for it to operate.

THE PROS
The Executive Committee—

- Can categorize the items submitted for addition to the agenda and ensure decision-making items are prioritized

- Ensures all board members are invited to submit items for the agenda

- Details the information needed by the board members prior to the board meeting to ensure all risks are addressed and options presented, and

- Ensures the CEO does not try to control what is placed on the agenda.

THE CONS
The Executive Committee may—

- Prioritize its own issues and place less weight on items submitted by other directors

- Fail to ensure that the board members have all the information they need to govern risks and debate the possible solutions/options

- Refuse to place items submitted by the board members on the agenda

- Try to strategically place items on the agenda (for example, if it is known that specific board members are unable to attend a meeting, this would make the item easier to deal with by the other board members), or

- Refuse to listen to the CEO's warnings that an item is of grave concern and needs to be addressed by the board as soon as possible.

The board's executive committee can promote cohesion among the full board or it can act as an entity unto itself and alienate other members. Thus, it is important to know how the executive committee functions before assigning it this role.

Where the executive committee operates as an independent entity, it may be better to assign the agenda setting function to the full board.

THE BOARD DESIGNS THE AGENDA

When the full board accepts responsibility for the agenda, it must dialogue and ensure all of its responsibilities are accepted. For example, the board ensures—

- The board's mandate is understood by all board members and the CEO; when the board members do not accept all aspects of it, the board designs a strategy to deal with this issue

- All members understand the difference between management and governance

- Governance policies are implemented and monitored

- Risks that are the responsibility of the board are monitored regularly via a board approved process

THE BOARD

ENSURES THE

- The roles of the board, its officers, its committees, and the CEO are written

MANDATE IS

UNDERSTOOD BY

- A strategic plan is crafted and progress monitored

ALL MEMBERS AND

- External influences that could impact on the work of the board are monitored

THE CEO

- Required reports are received, and

- Parliamentary procedures are followed.

There are clear pros and cons associated with board involvement in the agenda.

THE PROS
The board—

- Plans its work to ensure all responsibilities are completed as required

- Determines the information it needs to deal with all issues effectively and minimize risks

- Is fully informed and there are no surprises

- Is unable to blind side board members by placing items on the agenda when it is aware specific board members will be absent

- Works as a team, and

- Is positioned to speak with one voice, is in control of its work, and is not delegating its role to any staff member.

THE CONS
The board—

- Could fail to engage the CEO and find out about key issues too late, putting it in damage control mode, or

- Could fail to educate its board members about its role as one of governance and find itself dealing with minute issues, hence frustrating the CEO.

The more the board members are involved in the agenda setting, the more ownership they will have of the governance process.

FINAL COMMENT

The best boards plan their work to ensure that they demonstrate acceptance of their responsibilities and are in a position to leave a positive legacy at the end of their term. They work with the CEO but are not controlled by the CEO. The boards govern and ensure the CEO manages. Their policies and processes are clear. They are teams that can speak with one voice.

13—IS YOUR BOARD WORKING?

THE 12 HABITS OF INEFFECTIVE BOARD MEMBERS

Chairing a board or committee is a difficult job. It requires preparation, execution, and evaluation of every task. Unfortunately, chairpersons are unable to choose their teams, and may inherit or otherwise find themselves lumbered with troublesome or conflict-creating directors who undermine the board.

In other cases, directors are selected for a board because of their reputation or their friendships. These individuals may not always make the best board members or be up to the tasks asked of them.

Do you chair a board or committee and wonder why the group doesn't seem to accomplish goals? Are you a director who's fed up with meetings that drag on and never seem to accomplish anything or where co-directors push their own agendas?

BAD HABITS ARE DISRUPTIVE TO THE GROUP

This chapter is designed to assist chairpersons to identify the habits that may be disruptive to the harmony of the group. If you're the trouble-maker, this may be inadvertent and this chapter may open your eyes.

However, if you know you're doing your best to fulfill the responsibilities of a director, but the individual across the boardroom table is causing issues that chair and fellow directors seem unwilling or unable to resolve, is there anything you can do about it? Once the problem or problem-creator (even if it's you) is identified, it is possible to develop a strategy to restore harmony.

The 12 habits of ineffective board members are—

1. Desire to do only the minimum necessary
2. Inability to be cooperative
3. Inability to participate
4. Inappropriate backgrounds
5. Indecisiveness
6. Insufficient knowledge
7. Intolerance
8. Lack of commitment to the defined purpose or mandate
9. Lack of self will
10. Personal issues
11. Personality
12. Reliability

A board member may demonstrate one or more of these behaviors, yet everyone copes and adjusts. However, this may well be impacting your functionality as a board, and whether you achieve what you set out to do and fulfill your obligations. It may be time to find a solution.

Unfortunately, if you are the chairperson, you may have only one or two options. One is to identify the offending behavior and to address that issue with that board member. The second is to find a way to remove the person from the board or committee.

DO YOU RECOGNIZE YOURSELF?

If you're a director and think you may be showing some of these traits—it might be time to take a long and serious look at whether you're doing yourself more harm than good, on the board and off, with your approach. Professional executive guidance and coaching is often a good solution.

Sometimes, simply knowing when you're edging too close to the line is enough to modify your tendencies and help change your behavior.

If it's a fellow director exhibiting any of these traits to an unacceptable level to the point of impacting on board functions or its ability to reach goals, speak to the chair. Perhaps enlist the support of a fellow director to ensure that action is considered to remedy the issue.

1) DESIRE TO DO ONLY THE MINIMUM NECESSARY

There are individuals who want the position, but not the responsibility. They like the kudos, but may not like the work.

These members may or may not—
- Show up to meetings
- Read materials provided
- Contribute to the dialogue
- Refrain from forming sub-groups
- Refrain from politicking between meetings, or
- Say what they mean and mean what they say.

When board members are indifferent, they are not prepared to support the chairperson or the group. This situation has to be addressed on a one-to-one basis by the chair.

If this is you, be aware that your value as a board member may be limited.

2) INABILITY TO BE COOPERATIVE

Boards are based on a group model. Therefore, cooperation is the key to any board's success. Unfortunately, uncooperative behavior has a negative effect on any group. It can present in many forms:

- Argumentativeness

- Failure to complete assignments

- Unwillingness to work in a group model

- Silent rejection or refusal to cooperate with the decisions of the group

- Need to undermine others, or

- Need to be seen as superior.

If the behavior persists, the only way to correct this situation may be to find a way to remove the person from the board.

(Remember, this may be you. If these traits ring any bells, they could be affecting more than your business life. Some armchair therapy might be useful to explore what to do next. Read the books/talk to others, consider your actions as first steps to implementing change.)

3) INABILITY TO PARTICIPATE

There may be members who cannot contribute to the group for a series of reasons. They—

- Suffer from ill health

- Need to move location for work or other reasons

- Are required to fulfill family commitments, or

- Are unable to focus on issues when they do not have a personal interest in them.

These members cannot contribute to the group and may affect the chair's ability to obtain a quorum.

WHEN SHOULD INDIVIDUALS BE ASKED TO LEAVE THE BOARD?

One of the issues that will arise is whether individuals should be asked to leave a board when they are unable to fulfill their accepted role.

Many boards would like to ask members to resign when they do not put forth a 'good' reason for being unable to attend meetings. The problem occurs when the board is asked to define 'good' reason. It is a difficult task.

When the reason is ours—whether it's being away on business trips or a sick spouse— we will always think it's a good reason for missing the meetings. The key for the board is to determine when a member(s) absence affects the ability of the group to fulfill its obligations.

4) INAPPROPRIATE BACKGROUNDS

You may not have the option of choosing your board members. If you are the chair and you do have this authority, determine if the members have the talents required to assist the board to fulfill its mandate. If they do not, determine if and how you can remedy this situation.

5) INDECISIVENESS

Some people are unable to make decisions. These people may fear failure and may see failing as a reflection on their abilities or personality, rather than a way to learn for the next time.

They prolong decision making for as long as possible. This can be frustrating for other members, who know they have all of the data and information that's needed, have discussed the associated risks, and feel ready to make a decision and move to the next issue.

6) INSUFFICIENT KNOWLEDGE

Members may not have the knowledge to contribute to discussions. The board may not be willing to spend the money to provide the necessary professional development. Only the board can change this situation, unless a member is willing to take responsibility for his own education and is willing to fund this endeavor.

Guessing at the best solutions does nothing to enhance the credibility of a board. Board members need to hear 'the story' and attend to the facts prior to making any decision. Emotions are much stronger than facts, but they may not be as valid.

If you're a board member, you may need to take the time to do the learning curve on the industry or the tasks you'll be concerned with. However, keep in mind that this may not be quick enough and the talent may not be in your natural skill set or even attainable in a cost or time-effective framework.

7) INTOLERANCE

The close-minded board member may see everything from two vantage points—his own and/or from a negative perspective only. He may be unwilling to assimilate information that does not correlate with current opinions and may expend considerable energy putting down ideas, which he feels are not in harmony with his pre-conceived notions.

This board member may be short tempered when information is not consistent with his own. This person does not acquire new information easily and can put a strain on the group.

8) LACK OF COMMITMENT TO THE DEFINED PURPOSE/MANDATE

Individuals choose to become members for many reasons. The board may be an avenue to meet fellow directors. Other reasons include accepting the role as a favor for another person, to gain knowledge, to fulfill professional obligations, or to access perks.

If members choose to become directors for any of these reasons, they really do not want the role. The purpose is self-serving.

Boards need directors who can 'give' as well as 'take.' Usually, those whose philosophy is "what's in it for me?" are unable to focus on the good of the group and the assigned mandate because they are evaluating every task from their own perspective.

9) LACK OF SELF-WILL

Board members who have their own agenda or possess negative personal characteristics may be unwilling to focus on the agenda set for the group.

Board members who are involved in too many things may be unable to focus on the task at hand.

They do not refocus on the work of the board until they are in the next meeting. They are spread 'so thin' that they do not have the time or energy to devote to the work of the board.

Board members who behave in a manner distasteful to the other members are often unable or unwilling to change their tactics or contribute to the achievement of the goals of the group.

They are unable to see how their behavior negatively affects the group. Often, they do not care.

10) PERSONAL ISSUES

There may be personal issues interfering with a member's ability to contribute to the board or committee. These include disharmony in the board member's personal life and fear, such as fear of failure or rejection. These issues can be difficult to address because of an unwillingness to disclose personal information or they may be very deep-seated and require professional help or guidance to overcome.

11) PERSONALITY

There are individuals who are generally negative. This negativity can be expressed as—
- Finding fault
- Arguing over everything
- Focusing on minute details
- Intruding in areas that are not their concern
- Attacking others rather than focusing on the issues, or
- Refusing to respect the role of the chairperson.

These directors do not understand that power is associated with the cooperation of the group. The group decides on the agenda, remains within its mandate, determines risks, and is open to all ideas and options. It is not a matter of 'win-lose.' The success of the team depends on a 'win-win' philosophy.

12) RELIABILITY

Boards need to know that their members are honest. It is imperative that the position they present is open and reliable. When any board member says or does one thing in one setting but the direct opposite in another setting, the chairperson is always on guard. Unreliability can cause undue harm to the efforts of the board.

These members are unable to 'speak with one voice' after a decision is made. They may think they sound powerful when they criticize the board or its members. However, the behavior does nothing to support the board's efforts. Calculated unreliability is very disrespectful to the other board members. They would find it difficult to trust a fellow director who engages in such practices on an ongoing basis.

THE RESULT

When board members express the behaviors listed above, one of several things can happen.

Everyone is on guard. In fact, some of the board members may be relieved when certain members are unable to make a meeting.

The board is unable to follow a dispute resolution or problem solving process, thus disagreements go unresolved.

Focus shifts from the mandate to individuals.

The strategic plan does not get the attention it needs and at times it is only a wish list rather than a guide to achievable realistic goals.

The team fails to evaluate its effectiveness and definitely avoids the evaluation of its individual members.

Board members feel pressured to hold meetings outside of the regular meetings in order to avoid interaction with certain members.

The aggressive board members dominate discussions and other members feel obliged to remain silent if they have a different opinion.

AGGRESSIVE BOARD MEMBERS DOMINATE DISCUSSIONS AND OTHERS FEEL OBLIGED TO REMAIN SILENT

Decisions can be made before all of the data and information is collected, the options with their pros and cons are considered, and the risks evaluated.

Certain board members become disinterested because they do not want to deal with the ineffective board member.

All voices are not heard and certain persons/groups feel marginalized.

Personal attacks are not addressed and it is not possible to retain focus on the issues.

FINAL COMMENT

When choosing directors, or if you are a board member, consider the personal characteristics that are vital and most conducive to an effective team and creating a functional board.

ABOUT THE AUTHOR

Dr. Brenda Kelleher-Flight is the founder of GDP Consulting Inc., the creator of The Decision Making Model of Governance, and a leader in the field of governance, decision making, policy planning, and measurement for over 15 years.

For information, guidance, or advice on programs or services for your boardroom or organization,
please contact GDP Consulting Inc.
www.gdpconsulting.ca

www.ingramcontent.com/pod-product-compliance
Lightning Source LLC
Chambersburg PA
CBHW060619200326
41521CB00007B/816